weekends
with
the kids

weekends with the kids

activities * crafts * recipes

hundreds of ideas for family fun

sara perry

with kathlyn meskel

photographs by quentin bacon

CHRONICLE BOOKS
SAN FRANCISCO

Library of Congress Cataloging-in-Publication Data:

Perry, Sara.
Weekends with the kids : activities, crafts, recipes : hundreds of ideas for
family fun / by Sara Perry, with Kathlyn Meskel ; photographs by Quentin
Bacon.
          p. cm.
     ISBN 0-8118-3301-1
     1. Handicraft. 2. Cookery. I. Meskel, Kathlyn. II. Title.

TT157 .P455 2002
745.5—dc21   2001037179

Printed in Singapore

Craft development: Kathlyn Meskel
Craft and prop styling: Christina Wressell
Food styling: Darienne Sutton
Photographer's assistant: Tina Rupp
Designed by: Ariel Apte

Distributed in Canada by Raincoast Books
9050 Shaughnessy Street
Vancouver, British Columbia V6P 6E5

10 9 8 7 6 5 4 3 2 1

Chronicle Books LLC
85 Second Street
San Francisco, California 94105

www.chroniclebooks.com

dedication and acknowledgments

To Sofia Marie and Dylan Paul, and to Madeline Colleen and Jack Sinclaire,
who make our weekends the best times ever.

Thanks go to our friends and colleagues who generously shared their ideas, expertise, time,
and recipes, especially Jane Zwinger, Suzy Kitman, Sharon Maasdam, Fahti Rabizadeh, Bob Liner,
and Mikyla Bruder and Jodi Davis at Chronicle Books.
And to Catherine Glass, whose confidence and advice are always invaluable.

table
of
contents

introduction

Hooray! It's the weekend!

There's going to be time to wiggle our toes, play with our kids, and make every moment count. Sure, we've got errands to run and chores to get done, but there's also time for fun—for adventures, entertainment, crafts, quiet times, group activities, and very tasty food.

Let's face it, "weekends" don't always arrive Friday night. Sometimes they land in the middle of the week. Sometimes they're called school "in-service" days. And sometimes they're even called vacation. But whenever they happen and however long they last, we want days off from school to include good times with the kids.

Mom, dad, grandparent, uncle or aunt, friend of the family, or baby-sitter, you want this time to be happy, relaxing, refreshing, and memorable. But that's not always easy. Kids are full of energy, easily bored, and always hungry. You, on the other hand, would like to sleep in (fifteen more minutes, *please*), read the paper s-l-o-w-l-y, and have help fixing the meals. You'd also like to have a joyful time with your kids. *Weekends with the Kids* shows you how. It's a friendly handbook chock-full of engaging activities, tempting recipes, and creative ways for kids to spend time with you, as well as by themselves.

Here you'll find a game night, a living room camp-out, and a family dinner with lots of pizazz. You'll discover Incredibly Cool Clays, a Magnet-Maze Play Board, and Fun-in-the-Tub Toys. There are Secret Message Tubes, Under-the-Covers Flashlights, Wop-'em, Bop-'em Paddle Balls, and games of Funny-Paper Bingo. By now you're hungry, and the kids are starving, so pass the "Lettuce Forget the Bread" Sandwiches, the Seasoned-in-a-Snap Popcorn, and Everybody's Favorite Everything Cookie. When mealtime arrives, it will be hard to decide between Crazy-Crust Pizza and Pasta Bob. There's also a Mighty-Fine Meat Loaf with Barbecue Sauce. But save room for dessert. You'll have a hard time choosing between Fancy-Fingers Coconut and Ice-Cream Cake and S'more Sunday Sundaes.

fun snacks
and
quick eats

hairy pepper and the green goblet

When kids start creating these comical dip-and-dunk snacks, they end up munching veggies they've never tasted before. Curiosity gets the best of them. The more involved they get in the preparation, the more they end up eating. Start at the supermarket by letting the kids help you pick out the veggies and dips they know and love; then have them pick out one or two new ones. At home, they can decide what kind of characters to make following the general directions below.

makes **4** servings

1 small to medium yellow, red, or purple
    bell pepper, at room temperature

1 small to medium green bell pepper,
    at room temperature

1 to 1½ cups purchased or prepared dips,
    such as hummus, black bean dip,
    ranch dip, or yogurt dip

one 8-ounce can pasteurized process
    "spray" cheese spread

green and black sliced olives, sliced

celery slivers, slices, wedges, and sticks
    (see note)

radish slivers, slices, and wedges

red bell pepper slivers, slices,
    and wedges

broccoli florets and 3-inch stalks,
    sliced lengthwise

carrots, peeled, slivered, shredded,
    and cut into wedges and 5-inch
    sticks (see note)

peas

lettuce, shredded

cherry tomatoes, halved or quartered if
    necessary, or other small round fruit

cont'd . . .

✳ Rinse peppers. Using a clean kitchen towel, wipe the outside of each pepper dry. Carefully cut the top from each to form a cup. Discard the seeds and membranes. Fill each pepper one-half to two-thirds full of dip.

to make hairy pepper's face:

On the yellow pepper, using pea-sized balls of cheese spread, secure the eyes, nose, mouth, and ears in place. For eyes, use green or black sliced olives. For eyebrows, use celery slices, radish slices, or bell pepper slivers. For thicker brows, use tiny broccoli florets. For a nose, use a radish, carrot, or bell pepper wedge. For a mouth, use a radish or red bell pepper slice. (A steady hand with the cheese spread can add a pair of eyeglasses.)

to make the green goblet:

On the green pepper, using pea-sized balls of cheese spread, secure sparkling jewels made from whole peas and geometric shapes of celery, radishes, bell peppers, olives, and carrots. Using the cheese spread, create ribbons of gold around the goblet's rim and base.

✳ Arrange the peppers on a plate, and surround Hairy Pepper with a shredded carrot or lettuce collar. To make a bow tie, use slices of broccoli stalk or celery and a cherry tomato or other small round fruit for the knot. Using the cheese spread, add other decorative features. Just before serving, add Hairy Pepper's hair by inserting carrot and/or celery sticks halfway into the dip. For the green goblet's bubbling brew, press broccoli florets into the dip so that the tight heads are just showing.

→ note:

You will need 6 celery ribs, cut in half, to use as hair (dippers) and decorations. To make celery hair curly, cut 3 to 4 lengthwise slits, ⅛ inch apart, in one end of a celery stick. Submerge the cut ends in ice water for 5 to 10 minutes. Remove, and stick the straight ends into the dip. For wavy carrot hair, use a special wavy cutter, available where kitchen supplies are sold.

✳ To fill a pepper, you will need two 9-to-10-inch carrots, cut in half and then into sticks. For a shredded carrot collar, you will need 1 carrot.

sweet finger salad with romaine and mint

This refreshing, crisp finger salad appeals to children who want a cool, delicious dipping snack. Take it to an outdoor picnic at the park or serve it on your backyard patio. My Persian friend Fahti Rabizadeh gave me this recipe. She remembers it from her childhood in Tehran. During summer weekends, her family would gather on their rooftop garden and watch the evening stars fill up the sky.

serves 4

3 cups sugar

1 cup water

¾ cup white wine vinegar

2 bunches fresh mint leaves, washed and patted dry

Chilled inner leaves from 1 large head of romaine lettuce

* In a saucepan, combine the sugar and water. Bring the mixture to a boil over medium heat, stirring until the sugar dissolves. Simmer for 10 minutes. Add the vinegar, and continue to simmer until a medium syrup is formed, about 30 to 45 minutes.

* Stir in the mint, cover, and allow to steep until the syrup has cooled. Remove the mint, and pour syrup into a clean, dry bottle with a lid. The syrup can be served at room temperature or chilled. (If the syrup is too thick, thin by bringing it to room temperature and stirring in warm water, a teaspoon at a time.)

* To serve, arrange the lettuce leaves on a serving platter, or bundled into a wide-mouthed bowl or vase. Pour 1 cup syrup into a dipping bowl, and serve. Keep any unused syrup refrigerated for up to 1 month.

"lettuce forget the bread" sandwiches

Hooray, it's the weekend! Two days without that old familiar lunch sack. So forget the idea of a traditional sandwich, and let the gang experiment with these leafy lettuce roll-ups. They're a little like a burrito or pita bread pockets, just made for wrapping up your favorite filling. Look below, and "lettuce" choose the filling.

makes **4** sandwiches

> **4 outside iceberg lettuce leaves (see note)**
>
> **1 ⅓ cups shredded lettuce**
>
> **"Lettuce" Choose the Filling (recipe page 18)**
>
> **¼ cup purchased salad dressing or
>   Shake-It-Baby Dressing (page 43)**
>
> **4 lengths of kitchen string or party picks**

✳ On a plate, place the open leaves. Divide the shredded lettuce between the 4 leaves. Scatter or spoon ⅓ cup from each filling group over the shredded lettuce. Drizzle 1 tablespoon salad dressing over the mixture.

✳ Beginning at one end, wrap and roll each open leaf, and secure it with a length of kitchen string tied in the middle with a bow.

✳ (Sometimes the crisp leaves will crack. That's okay. If you wish, you can make a patch with another leaf and continuing rolling.) Or, secure rolls with party picks.

→ **note:**

For perfect lettuce leaves, cut off the bottom 1 inch from a medium-large head of iceberg. Core to a depth of 2 inches to release the leaves. Carefully peel away the large leaves.

cont'd...

"lettuce" choose the filling

From each group below, prepare one or
more ingredients by filling bowls or plates with
your selection. Each group should total at
least 1 ⅓ cups. Since you will be selecting
ingredients from each group to put into your
sandwiches, look for familiar (and not so familiar)
complementary flavors.

fruits or veggies:

chopped celery, cucumber, bell pepper, tomato,
avocado, apple, plum, or peach

grains or pasta:

cooked pasta, rice, couscous, cubed potato,
corn, white beans, or black beans

protein:

matchstick slices of cooked cubed chicken,
turkey, ham, meat loaf, egg, canned tuna,
tofu, or Cheddar, American, Jack, feta,
or mozzarella cheese

garnishes:

sliced olives, crumbled bacon, chopped
walnuts, chopped peanuts, chopped almonds,
raisins, dried cranberries, or granola

the big guy's favorite meat loaf sandwich

Here's a sandwich that's built for a laid-back weekend lunch. Stacked with great ingredients—homemade meat loaf, vine-ripe tomatoes, crispy bacon, your favorite sandwich bread, and zippy barbecue sauce—it's just the thing to keep you company while enjoying the Sunday paper or getting ready for an afternoon of outdoor fun.

makes **1** sandwich

2 slices good-quality white sandwich or
    sourdough bread, toasted

1 tablespoon mayonnaise or sandwich spread

1 tablespoon ketchup or homemade Barbecue
    Sauce (page 50)

½ cup torn butter lettuce or tender young
    arugula leaves

3 bacon slices, crisply cooked

2 or 3 Mighty-Fine Meat Loaf slices (page 50),
    ½-inch thick

1 medium vine-ripe tomato, cut into ¼-inch
    slices

＊ On each bread slice, spread an equal amount of mayonnaise. Spread the ketchup on 1 slice. Arrange half of the lettuce on the same slice, and top with the bacon. Arrange the remaining lettuce on the second slice, and top with the meat loaf and tomato slices. Press the bread slices together and cut in half.

the little guy's "me too" sandwich
Big guys aren't the only ones who like meat loaf for lunch. Kids do, too. And nothing's better than a slice squiggled with ketchup and mayo and sandwiched between their favorite bread. For a surprise, serve the sandwich open-faced, and top the meat with cheese-slice cutouts made using cookie-cutters.

＊ Or, create a pick-and-dip plate of treats. Cut the meat, cheese, and bread into chunks, or use a garnish-cutter to make fun shapes. Serve with a bowl of ketchup or barbeque sauce and let the kids pick and dip their way through a nutritious snack.

"quick! i'm hungry" sandwich ideas

During the week, the slap-it-together sandwich is just fine for schoolyard lunches and desk-side meals, but on the weekend it's time for a change. Below you'll find some simple sandwich ideas to keep pace with your weekend plans.

1 Use an imaginative substitute for sliced bread: a tortilla, pita bread, lavash, bagel, croissant, hot dog or hamburger bun, crackers (don't forget graham), or an English muffin. Use standard fillings you know the kids like, as well as some favorite foods they've never tried in a sandwich. Stuff a pita with yesterday's spaghetti and meat sauce, or fill a tortilla with shredded carrot, raisin, and walnut salad and roll it up for a veggie sandwich.

2 Use cookie-cutters to transform a sliced-bread sandwich into whimsical figures and other shapes. For easy assembly, first cut the bread into desired shapes, then spread with fillings.

3 Use a paring knife to transform a plain sandwich into a puzzle by cutting it into several unusual pieces. It sure beats cutting a sandwich in half!

4 Make tube-shaped sandwiches by removing the crusts from a slice of sandwich bread. Spread with a thin filling such as peanut butter and jelly or mayonnaise and thinly sliced meat or cheese and roll, jellyroll fashion, into a tube.

5 Open-faced sandwiches take on their own personality when kids use them as a palette for edible characters or designs.

6 Make muffin men from toasted English muffins. First spread a smooth filling such as peanut butter or spaghetti sauce across the muffin. Decorate with faces made from grated cheese, squeezable jams or ketchups (have you tried the green ketchup?), sliced olives, slivered pickles, and any condiment you can conjure up.

7 Critter crackers come together in a breeze using oblong or round crackers for the bodies, peanut butter or squeezable cheese spread for "glue,"

knot-shaped pretzels for wings, and sliced and diced pickles, olives, and other raw veggies for eyes and body parts. Or, using any of the above ingredients, make free-form modernistic designs fit for a budding artist.

8 Nothing beats the taste of a peanut butter sandwich, especially when it's paired with a favorite jam or a combination of silly but savory toppings.

First set out some of the toppings described on the right. Have the kids spread 2 slices of bread with peanut butter. Then, let them put 1, 2, or 3 toppings on 1 slice of bread. It's also fun to put 1 kind of topping on 1 half of the bread and a different topping or combination on the other half. Set the remaining bread slice on top, press gently, and cut the sandwich in half lengthwise. Whose half sandwich tastes best? Which one has the most unusual combination?

toppings:

American cheese slices, pineapple rings, raisins, crisply cooked bacon, sliced sweet pickles, sliced bananas (plain or sprinkled with brown sugar), granola, egg salad, tuna fish salad, and, last but not least, fruit jams and jellies.

For a quick-as-a-wink tuna or egg salad filling, combine 1 drained 6-ounce can tuna in water or 3 chopped hard-cooked eggs with 2 tablespoons mayonnaise or Miracle Whip Salad Dressing and 2 teaspoons sweet relish until blended. Want some crunch? Add a little chopped celery.

pssst:

Peanut butter not your thing? Then try the experiment with an open-faced grilled cheese sandwich.

seasoned-in-a-snap popcorn

You can season and flavor popcorn with just about anything. It can be a wholesome snack or a sugar-sweet treat that's just the ticket for a Friday night video. Bring it as a munch-along snack on a hike, or leave it as a fly-by grab at the kitchen counter.

In the following recipes, unless noted, 1 bag of plain microwave popcorn is used. Each bag serves 2 and equals about 10 cups, or 2½ quarts, popped corn.

flavored-sugar popcorn

Sprinkle just-popped popcorn with one of the following flavored sugars: cinnamon sugar (3 teaspoons ground cinnamon mixed with ¼ cup sugar), chocolate sugar (¼ cup unsweetened cocoa powder such as Droeste with ¼ cup sugar), or, for a little zip, Chinese five-spice sugar (2 to 4 teaspoons Chinese five-spice powder with ¼ cup sugar).

taco-time popcorn

Melt 2 tablespoons butter and stir in 1 to 1¼ teaspoons taco seasoning. Drizzle immediately on just-popped popcorn, and season with salt if desired.

parmesan popcorn

Melt 2 tablespoons butter, and stir in ½ teaspoon fresh lemon juice. Drizzle immediately on just-popped popcorn. Sprinkle with grated parmesan, tossing it, and season with salt if desired.

g.o.r.p.p.!!

This is an abbreviation for "good old raisins and peanuts plus popcorn." In a large bowl, combine 1 cup dry-roasted peanuts with 1 cup dark or golden raisins. In batches, toss in 5 cups popped corn, warm or room temperature, until all the ingredients are well blended. For added pleasure, stir in M&M's or other coated chocolate candies as well as dried cranberries, mini-pretzels, or mini-marshmallows. Plain goldfish or tiny teddy bear crackers are terrific, too.

cont'd...

candy-nut crunch

Preheat the oven to 300°F. Coat a roasting pan or rimmed baking sheet with nonstick spray, and distribute 1 bag popped corn and 1 cup salted Spanish peanuts, almonds, or other salty nuts on it. In a medium saucepan, mix ⅔ cup packed dark or light brown sugar, 2 tablespoons unsalted butter, 2 tablespoons clear corn syrup, and 2 tablespoons vegetable oil together until blended. Over medium heat, cook and stir until the mixture boils. Without stirring, cook undisturbed for 5 minutes.

✳ Remove from heat, and stir in ½ teaspoon ground cinnamon, 2 teaspoons vanilla, ⅛ teaspoon baking soda, and ⅓ cup raisins. Pour mixture over popcorn mixture, stirring gently to coat. Bake until golden brown, 20 to 25 minutes. Cool on a large piece of buttered aluminum foil. Serves 4.

caramel ginger cashew spice crunch

This is made for a grown-up craving. Preheat the oven to 300°F. Coat a roasting pan or rimmed baking sheet with nonstick spray, and distribute 1 bag popped corn and 1½ cups salted almonds on it. In a medium saucepan, mix ⅔ cup packed dark or light brown sugar, 2 tablespoons unsalted butter, 2 tablespoons clear corn syrup, and 2 tablespoons toasted sesame oil together until blended. Over medium heat, cook and stir until the mixture boils. Without stirring, cook undisturbed for 5 minutes.

✳ Remove from heat, and stir in ½ teaspoon white pepper, ½ teaspoon ground cinnamon, 1 teaspoon ginger powder, 2 teaspoons vanilla, ⅛ teaspoon baking soda, ¼ cup chopped crystallized ginger, and ⅓ cup coarsely chopped dried cherries. Pour mixture over popcorn mixture, stirring gently to coat. Bake until golden brown, 20 to 25 minutes. Cool on a large piece of buttered aluminum foil. Serves 4.

rocky-road marshmallow crispies

Let's be truthful: weekends are for splurging on treats that everyone loves—those old-fashioned goodies that keep getting gobbled up before they've had a chance to settle in the pan. This rendition of the no-bake rice cereal treat erupts with milk chocolate chips, semisweet chocolate chips, butterscotch chips, and toasted almonds. Your kids can help you measure the ingredients and smoosh the sticky mixture into the pan.
Oh—and if you make this Friday night, stash a few so you have enough for a mid-afternoon Saturday coffee break.

makes about **4 1/2** dozen squares

4 tablespoons unsalted butter

**5 cups (10 ounces) mini-marshmallows or
50 large marshmallows**

**6 cups puffed rice cereal, such as Rice
Krispies**

1 1/2 cups whole toasted almonds (see note)

1/3 cup frozen milk chocolate chips (see note)

1/2 cup frozen semisweet chocolate chip

1/3 cup frozen butterscotch chips

cont'd...

* Heavily coat a 13-by-9-by-2-inch baking pan with nonstick spray. Coat a spatula with nonstick spray.

* In a 2½- to-3-quart heavy saucepan, melt the butter over low heat. Add the marshmallows, and stir until completely melted and the mixture begins to bubble, about 5 minutes. Remove from the heat, and immediately add the rice cereal.

* Gently stir until coated. Stir in the almonds and chocolate and butterscotch chips until blended. The mixture will be sticky. Using the spatula, press the rice cereal mixture into the pan.

* Allow the mixture to set, about 3 hours (if your hungry snackers can wait that long). Using the spatula, loosen the entire pan of crispies, and invert onto a cutting board before cutting into 1½-inch squares. (If hunger rules the day, forgo this step and cut the squares directly from the pan. They will not be as pretty but will taste just as good.)

→ note:

To toast almonds, preheat the oven to 350°F. Spread the nuts on a rimmed baking sheet, and bake until lightly browned, 8 to 10 minutes.

* The chips are frozen to keep them from melting in the warm cereal mixture.

chocolate-chocolate marshmallow crispies:

For chocolate lovers, follow the recipe for Rocky-Road Marshmallow Crispies, substituting 4½ cups mini-marshmallows and ½ cup Nutella hazelnut-chocolate spread or other chocolate spread for the 5 cups mini-marshmallows. Also, substitute ⅓ cup frozen white chocolate chips for the ⅓ cup frozen butterscotch chips.

snicker-snack granola

Before the weekend arrives, stir up a batch of this terrific-tasting granola to use for morning cereal or weekend munchies. For breakfast, you may want to leave out the dried fruit and add fresh berries or a sliced banana to the bowl. If the kids want to take this snack along on a backpack adventure, let them make up their own concoction by adding their favorite dried fruits, nuts, and chocolate- or yogurt-covered goodies.

makes about **6** cups

plain granola:

3 cups old-fashioned rolled oats

1 cup slivered almonds

1 cup shredded sweetened coconut

½ cup sesame seeds

¼ cup wheat germ (optional)

6 tablespoons pure maple syrup

¼ cup plus 2 tablespoons light brown sugar, firmly packed

¼ cup vegetable oil

2 tablespoons warm water

¼ teaspoon salt

dried fruit choices:

1 cup golden raisins, or

⅓ cup chopped dried apricots,

⅓ cup chopped dark or golden raisins, and

⅓ cup chopped dried dates

cont'd...

to bake the plain granola:

Preheat the oven to 300°F. Grease a rimmed baking sheet with nonstick spray.

* In a large bowl, combine the rolled oats, almonds, coconut, sesame seeds, and wheat germ, if desired. In a small bowl, whisk the maple syrup, brown sugar, oil, water, and salt together until blended. Pour the syrup mixture over the rolled-oat mixture, and stir to combine. Spread the mixture evenly in the prepared pan. Bake for 45 minutes or until evenly browned, stirring every 10 to 15 minutes. Transfer the pan to a wire rack to cool.

to add the dried fruit

After cooling, transfer the baked granola to a large bowl, and stir in the desired fruit. Store in an airtight container.

snicker-snack chocolate chunks

For those who know there's never enough chocolate, follow the recipe for plain Snicker-Snack Granola. Coat a cookie sheet with nonstick spray, and line it with waxed paper. Melt 4 ounces milk chocolate chips or a 4-ounce candy bar in the top of a double boiler. When the chips have just melted, remove from the heat, and stir until smooth. Add ¾ cup Snicker-Snack Granola and ¼ cup golden raisins, and stir until thoroughly combined. Drop by walnut-sized teaspoonfuls onto the waxed paper. Set aside to cool and set. Makes 16 to 18 cookies.

everybody's favorite everything cookie

In our house, every time this cookie gets made, it turns out a little different. That's because it depends on who's measuring the ingredients. If it's a raisin-lover, dark and golden raisins get mixed together. If it's a chocolate fiend, chips galore! (And if it's me, more granola.) You can't go wrong as long as the basic dough ingredients remain the same and the goodies are kept in proportion. See what great combinations your family comes up with. But please try this version first.

makes about **4** dozen cookies

basic dough:

¾ cup all-purpose flour

½ teaspoon baking powder

¼ teaspoon baking soda

¼ teaspoon salt

¾ cup (1 ½ sticks) unsalted butter, at room temperature

½ cup sugar

½ cup light brown sugar, firmly packed

2 teaspoons vanilla extract

1 egg, at room temperature

1 cup old-fashioned rolled oats

goodies:

1 cup Snicker-Snack Granola (page 28), purchased granola, or crushed cereal

¾ cup sweetened shredded coconut, lightly packed

½ to ¾ cup toasted chopped pecan bits or other chopped nuts

1 cup white chocolate chips or other flavored chips or coated candies made for baking

½ cup golden raisins or dark raisins, currants, dried cranberries, or other chopped dried fruits

cont'd...

* Preheat the oven to 375°F. Set aside 2 ungreased or parchment-lined baking sheets.

For the basic dough:
In a bowl, whisk the flour, baking powder, baking soda, and salt together until blended.

* In another bowl, using an electric mixer on medium speed, beat the butter and sugars until light and fluffy, about 5 minutes. Beat in the vanilla. Add the egg, and beat until blended, about 1 minute. Add the flour mixture, ½ cup at a time, until blended and no flour shows. Stir in the rolled oats.

For the added goodies:
Stir in the granola, coconut, nuts, chocolate chips, and dried fruit. Beat on low speed until blended.

* Drop by rounded tablespoonfuls onto a baking sheet, leaving at least 1 inch between each mound of dough. For chewy cookies, bake until light golden, about 10 minutes. For crisp cookies, bake until golden brown all over, about 14 minutes. Cool slightly on the baking sheet before transferring to a wire rack, or carefully pull the parchment paper from the pan and place it, along with the cookies, on the wire rack. Store in an airtight container.

no-more-homework chocolate soda

Weekend homework. Yuck.

Getting it all done. Cool.

The perfect reward. Slurp, slurp.

makes **1** soda

3 tablespoons chilled chocolate-flavored syrup

2 tablespoons chilled milk

½ to ¾ cup chilled club soda or seltzer water

1 large scoop vanilla ice cream

sweetened whipped cream

chocolate curls (see note)

1 maraschino cherry

＊ In a 12-ounce chilled glass, combine the chocolate syrup and chilled milk. Add enough club soda to fill the glass three-fourths full, and stir. Add the vanilla ice cream, and top with more club soda. Top with sweetened whipped cream, chocolate curls, and a maraschino cherry.

→ **note:**

To make chocolate curls, unwrap your favorite chocolate and hold the bar with a towel or waxed paper so the warmth of your hand won't melt it. Pressing a potato peeler firmly against the horizontal side of the bar, pull along the chocolate in long strokes, creating curls as you go.

variation:

For a subtle, fruit-flavored soda, decrease the chocolate syrup to 2 tablespoons and substitute fruit-flavored carbonated spring water. Proceed as directed. For a more intense chocolate flavor, use chocolate milk and chocolate ice cream. Proceed as directed.

"quick! i'm thirsty" drink ideas

When they're thirsty and want something special, and you're in a hurry and short on ideas, try one of the following delectable drinks. For a sweet surprise, create swell straws using fresh licorice whips with their ends snipped off, or hand them super swizzle-sticks made from peppermint or candy sticks.

weekend bubbly

In a tall glass, combine apple, cranberry, or other fruit juices with club soda, fruit-flavored soda, ginger ale, or 7-Up-style sodas.

kaleidoscope koolers

Next time the kids are thirsty, set out clear plastic glasses, plain or flavored sparkling water, and a bowl filled with ice cubes made with all those "last of the juices." They can mix and match ice cubes, and watch the colors blend and blur.

good-for-you float

Instead of plain milk with lunch, make it a float by adding a scoop or two of frozen yogurt or ice cream in a favorite flavor. For a little pizzazz, tint the milk with a few drops of food coloring. Or shake in some colored sugar sprinkles.

peanut butter and strawberry jam smoothie

Forget the sandwich—make their PB&J a cool and creamy milkshake. In a blender, combine ¼ cup milk, 1 cup vanilla ice cream or frozen yogurt, 1 tablespoon smooth peanut butter, and 5 strawberries or 1 tablespoon strawberry jam. Blend until smooth, beginning at low speed and increasing speed a little as the mixture begins to whirl. Pour into a tall glass and serve. Makes 1.

creamy-dreamy orange smoothie

In a blender, combine ¼ cup milk, 1 cup vanilla ice cream or frozen yogurt, 1 cup orange sorbet or sherbet, and 2 tablespoons frozen orange juice concentrate. Blend until smooth, beginning at low speed and increasing speed a little as the mixture begins to whirl. Pour into a tall glass, and serve. Makes 1.

family meals
and
sleep-in breakfasts

crazy-crust pizza

Moms and dads, and even grandparents, will remember this crazy crust from when they were young. It's been around for a long time. That's because it's easy and good, and kids love to make it. Just be sure to sprinkle on the meat before the first baking. It helps even out the dough and keep it flat. As with any pizza, you can alter or add extra toppings. This is my family's favorite.

makes **1** twelve-inch pizza

dough:

1 cup all-purpose flour

1 teaspoon dried Italian seasoning or oregano

1 teaspoon salt

½ teaspoon garlic powder

pinch of black pepper

2 eggs, lightly beaten

⅔ cup milk

topping:

1 pound chicken or pork Italian sausage or ground beef

¼ cup chopped onion

1 cup pizza, marinara, or tomato sauce

one 2.25-ounce can sliced black olives, drained (optional)

1 cup thinly sliced pepperoni (optional)

2 roma tomatoes, sliced (optional)

1 to 1½ cups shredded mozzarella cheese

cont'd...

to make the dough:

Preheat the oven to 425°F. Coat a 12-inch pizza pan with nonstick spray, dust with flour or cornmeal, and set aside.

✳ In a medium bowl, whisk the flour, Italian seasoning, salt, garlic powder, and pepper together until blended. Stir in the eggs and milk until combined. The dough will resemble a thick batter. Pour the batter onto the prepared pan, spreading it evenly.

to make the topping:

Meanwhile, in a medium skillet, sauté the sausage and onion over medium heat until the meat is browned. Drain off any excess liquid or fat. Using a slotted spoon, evenly distribute the meat mixture over the batter. Bake until the crust is golden brown, 20 to 25 minutes. Remove from oven. Spread the pizza sauce on top. Sprinkle the olives and arrange the pepperoni and tomatoes over the sauce, if desired, and sprinkle with cheese. Bake until the cheese melts, about 10 minutes. Cut into wedges, and serve.

✳ Leftover slices freeze well covered with plastic wrap. Reheat in a toaster oven.

tossed green salad with shake-it-baby dressing

When a busy weekend leaves little time for kitchen routines, here's a little help from your supermarket. One of the most convenient produce items to come along is packaged, ready-to-serve organic salad greens. Triple-washed, crisp, and flavorful, they're a sanity-saver. The 5-to-7-ounce bags are enough for 4 small servings (don't let the size of the bag fool you; the greens expand in the bowl) and come in mixed greens, baby spinach, romaine, and other assortments. Let your kids mix up the salad dressing. Set out a 1-pint jar with a tight-fitting lid, measuring spoons, a measuring cup, and their favorite fixings.

serves 4

one 5-to-7-ounce package organic
    salad greens, about 6 cups

1 cup purchased croutons

½ cup Shake-It-Baby Salad Dressing
    (recipes follow)

shake-it-baby salad dressing #1:
makes ¾ cup dressing

½ cup olive oil

¼ cup red or white vinegar

½ teaspoon Dijon mustard

1 additional option (see "optional
    ingredients," page 44)

Salt and pepper

shake-it-baby salad dressing #2:
makes ¾ cup dressing

½ cup light sour cream

2 tablespoons mayonnaise

1 tablespoon milk

1 tablespoon rice wine vinegar

½ teaspoon garlic powder

1 additional option (see "optional
    ingredients," page 44)

Salt and pepper

cont'd...

optional ingredients:

2 to 3 tablespoons crumbled blue cheese;
or 2 to 3 tablespoons shredded Parmesan
cheese and ¼ teaspoon Worcestershire
sauce; or 1 to 2 teaspoons maple syrup or
honey; or 2 tablespoons minced green onion
and ½ teaspoon grated orange zest

shake-it-baby salad dressing #1

In a 1-pint container with a tight-fitting lid,
add the oil, vinegar, and mustard. Add an
optional ingredient if desired. Fasten lid
securely, and shake it, baby, until blended.
Season with salt and pepper to taste.

shake-it-baby salad dressing #2

In a 1-pint container with a tight-fitting lid,
add the sour cream, mayonnaise, milk, vinegar,
and garlic powder. Add an optional ingredient,
if desired. Fasten the lid securely, and shake it,
baby, until blended. Season with salt and pepper
to taste.

to make the salad:

In a large salad bowl, gently toss the salad by
lifting and mixing the greens and the croutons.
Pour two-thirds of the dressing over the salad
mixture, and toss to blend. Taste, adding
more dressing if necessary. Serve immediately.

tv-tray nibblers

For kids only. Shhhhhhh, let the grown-ups snooze and sleeping dogs dream. Put together a tray of treats to eat in front of your favorite cartoons. Don't forget those swirly frozen lollipops in the freezer, the jam-filled muffins defrosting on the counter, and that box of waffle ice-cream cones you can turn into a super dessert like breakfast.

for frozen lollipop fruit swirls you will need:

**wooden craft or Popsicle sticks or skewers
(6 or 8 inches long)**

canned pineapple slices, drained

**yogurt, preferably with two flavors in each
container, such as Yoplait's Trix**

frozen lollipop fruit swirls

These cool, swirly lollipops look more like carnival candy than part of a nutritious breakfast. Made from pineapple slices and kid-friendly yogurt, they take minutes to create and pop in the freezer, ready to grab at a hungry moment's notice.

✳ Line a baking sheet with waxed paper, and set aside. For each lollipop, push a stick or skewer through a pineapple slice widthwise and through its center hole. (If the pineapple is fragile, use a paring knife to make a small slit in which to insert the stick.) Spoon 2 tablespoons yogurt onto the waxed paper. With the back of the spoon, swirl the yogurt into a circle slightly larger than the pineapple slice. Gently press the pineapple into the yogurt. Spread 2 more tablespoons yogurt over the top and down the sides of the fruit. Freeze until the yogurt hardens, 2 to 3 hours.

✳ To remove, gently peel off the paper. (For a finished look, use a small knife to run an even outline around the fruit before removing it from the waxed paper.) Wrap in a sandwich-sized plastic bag or in foil. Freeze for up to 1 month.

cont'd . . .

banana-rama-ding-dongs

Peel a banana and cut it in half. Insert a wooden stick or skewer into each cut end. Dip in your favorite flavored yogurt, and roll in granola, cereal, chopped nuts, or chocolate chips. Lay on a waxed paper–lined baking sheet, and freeze for 2 hours. To remove, gently peel off the paper. Wrap in sandwich-sized plastic bags or in foil. Freeze for up to 1 month. Makes 2.

in-my-jammy jammies

Follow the recipe for Sweet Polenta Muffins (page 62). Spoon 1 heaping tablespoon batter into each of the prepared muffin cups, smoothing it out with a clean finger. Spoon 1 teaspoon fruit jam on top of each portion of batter, and top with the remaining batter, dividing it among the muffin cups. Gently spread the top batter so that no jam shows. Bake until golden, about 30 minutes. Let cool in the pan for 5 minutes, and then transfer to a wire rack to finish cooling. Remember, the jam stays hot for some time. Check before serving so that young mouths don't get burned.

creamy jammy jammies

Follow the recipe for In-My-Jammy Jammies. Place a ¼-to-½-teaspoon-sized chunk of cream cheese in with the jam, and proceed as directed. The creamy center does not melt, and it tastes terrific with the jam.

"quick! i'm watching cartoons" breakfast ideas

dippity-do frosted fruit tray

On a tray, prepare a plate of easy-to-handle fresh fruit, such as apple wedges, banana chunks, and small bunches of grapes. Serve them with a carton of yogurt for dipping. For a crunchy fruit munchy, dip the yogurt-covered fruit into a bowl of granola or crushed cereal.

dippity-do fancy fruit parfait

In a parfait or deep-stemmed glass, using the same ingredients as the Dippity-Do Frosted Fruit Tray (recipe above), alternate fresh fruit chunks with spoonfuls of yogurt and a sprinkling of granola or crushed cereal. Create several layers for a festive, fruity breakfast.

on-the-go waffle cone

Spread 1 tablespoon creamy peanut butter on the inside of a waffle cone. Fill the cone with one 8-ounce container custard-style yogurt. Top with sliced bananas, strawberries, or raspberries.

bowl-me-over

Mix 3 or 4 different dry cereals together, and see what the combination tastes like.

muffin à la mode

Serve a warm breakfast muffin with a small scoop of frozen vanilla yogurt. Top with warm strawberry jam or other fruit preserves.

nibble necklaces, bracelets, or lariats

Thread O-shaped cereals such as Cheerios, Froot Loops, Apple Jacks, and Grape-Nut O's onto lengths of clean kitchen string (or, if grown-ups aren't watching, licorice whips). Tie the crispy creations into necklaces, bracelets, or lariats.

mighty-fine meat loaf with barbecue sauce

This is a mighty-fine meat loaf for many reasons. Take, for instance, the wonderful aroma. It fills the house with promises of things to come. Or the great flavor kids of all ages adore. But the real sensation is the sweet-and-spicy barbecue sauce. Not only do you add it to the meat loaf before it bakes, you can use it as a sauce afterward. So be prepared: make a second batch, because you'll get requests for more sauce to use like gravy, as a dip, or as a spread on the Big Guy's Favorite Meat Loaf Sandwich (page 19). When baked, this dish will give off less drippings than a traditional meat loaf. That's because lean beef and sausage are used to help reduce the fat (and no one will taste the difference). That's mighty fine in my book.

serves 8 to 10

barbecue sauce:

¼ teaspoon black pepper

¼ teaspoon ground cumin

¼ teaspoon ground cinnamon

¼ teaspoon ground allspice

1 teaspoon garlic powder

pinch to ¼ teaspoon mild chili powder

pinch to ¼ teaspoon cayenne pepper

½ cup ketchup

2 tablespoons Dijon mustard

3 tablespoons molasses, light or dark

2 tablespoons honey

meat loaf:

1 small onion, chopped

1 small celery stalk, diced

1 medium carrot, shredded

1 tablespoon olive oil

½ teaspoon minced garlic

1 pound lean ground beef

1 pound ground chicken, turkey, or lean pork sausage

⅓ cup old-fashioned rolled oats

¼ cup finely chopped parsley

1 egg, lightly beaten

✳ Preheat the oven to 350°F.

to make the sauce:

In a medium sauté pan, combine the black pepper, cumin, cinnamon, allspice, garlic powder, chili powder, and cayenne. Over medium-high heat, heat the spices until they release their aromas and a whiff of smoke appears, 1 to 2 minutes. Do not let burn. Stir in the ketchup, mustard, molasses, and honey, and cook over medium heat until blended and heated through. Set aside to cool.

to make the meat loaf:

In a large sauté pan, sauté the onion, celery, and carrot in olive oil over medium-high heat until limp, stirring constantly, 3 to 5 minutes. Add the garlic, and continue to sauté until fragrant, about 1 minute. Set aside to cool.

✳ In a large bowl, add the ground beef, sausage, sautéed vegetables, ½ cup barbecue sauce, rolled oats, and parsley. With 2 forks, rake and toss the mixture until combined. Add the egg, and blend again. The mixture will be moist. Gently form into a rectangular shape, and transfer to a 9-by-13-inch baking pan. Bake for 45 minutes.

✳ Open the oven door, remove the meat, and coat the top with barbecue sauce. Return to oven, and continue to bake for another 30 to 40 minutes, or until meat thermometer inserted in the middle reads 155°F. Using 2 spatulas, lift the meat loaf out of the pan and onto the serving platter. Let the meat rest for 10 minutes before serving. Pass additional barbecue sauce.

make mine mashed potatoes

Don't even think about it. No rice, no noodles, not even a baked potato. When it comes to a meat loaf dinner, mashed potatoes will win out every time, especially these.

serves 4

2 pounds Idaho or baking potatoes, peeled and cut into large cubes

2 tablespoons whole milk, warmed

3 tablespoons unsalted butter

1 cup (3 ½ to 4 ounces) shredded Fontina cheese

coarse (kosher) salt and pepper

saturday night dinner

* In a large saucepan, cover the cubed potatoes with cold water. Bring to a boil over medium-high heat. Reduce the heat to a slow boil, and cook until the potatoes are tender, 20 to 30 minutes. Drain for 1 to 2 minutes, letting the steam rise and the potatoes dry out.

* Put the potatoes through a ricer or food mill into a large mixing bowl or the saucepan. Add the milk and butter, and beat until smooth. Stir in the cheese until it melts. Season with salt and pepper to taste, and serve immediately.

fancy-fingers coconut and ice-cream cake

You'll have fun putting together this cake-and-ladyfinger extravaganza, and so will the kids. It looks like a jewel box or a pirate's chest. Let the kids decorate the ladyfingers with zigzag patterns, tic-tac-toe stripes, and lots of sprinkles and decorative candies. Vary the decorations on each ladyfinger, then stand them up side-by-side on the cake to resemble a fence. For even more pizzazz, decorate the top with colorful candies. Oh yes, the cake tastes good, especially when you bite into the ice-cream layer.

serves **6** to **8**

½-gallon block vanilla ice cream

20 purchased biscuitlike ladyfingers, 1-by-4½ inches each

decorating icing tubes (4.25 ounces each), in assorted colors

decorating gel icing tubes (4.25 ounces each), in assorted colors

decorating sprinkles, confetti, and candies, in assorted colors

1 frozen Pepperidge Farm 3-Layer Coconut Cake (1.2 pounds)

to prepare the ice-cream layer:
Place the ice-cream block on a cutting board. Warm the blade of a large, heavy knife under hot water. Cut the ice-cream in half horizontally. On a flat baking sheet or platter, place the 2 halves side-by-side and touching. To "glue" the halves together, run the knife blade under hot water, and run it along the 2 sides that are touching. Press the sides together. Using the warm knife blade, trim the ice cream to fit the bottom of the frozen cake. Cover the ice cream with plastic wrap, and freeze until firm.

to decorate the ladyfingers:
Use decorating icings, gels, and sprinkles to decorate the top (rounded) side of each ladyfinger. Set aside on a baking sheet.

cont'd...

to assemble and serve:

Remove the coconut cake from its package. Thaw in the refrigerator about 3 hours or at room temperature for 1 to 1½ hours. On a dessert platter, squeeze several dollops of decorative frosting in the center. Center the prepared ice-cream layer in the middle of the platter, pressing down gently to secure it to the frosting. (This will keep the ice cream from shifting.) Set the cake on top of the ice cream. Decorate the sides of the cake with the decorated ladyfingers, 5 to a side, by gently pressing into the frosting. The ladyfingers will cover the sides of both the ice cream and the cake. Serve immediately.

really good oatmeal pancakes

This wholesome batter creates cakes that are light and cakey and have a mild flavor, kissed with cinnamon, that kids love. For best results, it's important to let the oatmeal soak overnight in the buttermilk. (I have been known to shortcut this step by warming the buttermilk and soaking the oatmeal for an hour or two in the morning.) You'll find some appealing variations below, including a currant-studded pancake and a crepelike roll-up filled with sour cream and sweet jam. For kids on the run, there's a wrap-and-roll version they can fill with yogurt or peanut butter and jelly before heading off to try their luck at Funny-Paper Bingo (page 104).

makes **8** four-inch pancakes and **1** tester

1 cup old-fashioned rolled oats	Pinch of salt
1 cup buttermilk	1 egg, at room temperature
¼ cup all-purpose flour	2 tablespoons melted butter, butter for serving
1 to 2 tablespoons sugar	warm maple syrup for serving
½ teaspoon baking powder	sliced fresh fruits for decorating
½ teaspoon baking soda	containers of squeezable jam for decorating
½ teaspoon ground cinnamon	

the night before:
In a medium bowl, mix the rolled oats and buttermilk together until blended. Cover and refrigerate.

＊ In a medium bowl, whisk the flour, sugar, baking powder, baking soda, cinnamon, and salt together until blended. Cover and set aside.

cont'd...

to prepare the pancakes:

In a large bowl, combine the oatmeal-buttermilk mixture, egg, and melted butter. Stir in the flour mixture until blended. The batter will be thick.

* Coat a griddle or electric skillet with nonstick spray. Preheat to 350°F or medium for 5 minutes. For each cake, pour ¼ cup batter onto the heated griddle. With the back of a spoon, gently spread the batter into a 4-inch circle. Cook until top is bubbly and the cake is dry around the edges. Flip over, and cook until golden on both sides.

* Serve with butter and warm maple syrup, or decorate the pancakes, making faces and designs with cut fruit slices and jams.

oatmeal currant pancakes

Follow the recipe for Really Good Oatmeal Pancakes. In a small bowl or cup, marinate 3 to 4 tablespoons currants in ¼ cup warm orange juice for 10 minutes. Drain, and stir into the batter before cooking.

fancy sunday morning roll-ups

Taste, texture, and eye-popping appeal make these pancakes the hit of any weekend brunch. Follow the recipe for Really Good Oatmeal Pancakes, adding ¼ cup milk to the batter after the dry ingredients are added. Working in batches, pour ⅓ cup batter onto a hot round skillet. (On a griddle, pour batter in a 10-inch strip.)

* When the pancake is cooked, remove and spread 2 tablespoons of your favorite jam or preserve over the pancake, leaving a ½-inch rim. Spoon 3 tablespoons sour cream along the center. Roll up in jellyroll fashion, and top with a dollop of sour cream, a dollop of jam, and a garnish of fresh fruit, such as raspberries, blueberries, or a sliced strawberry. Dust with powdered sugar, and serve.

wrap-and-roll pancakes

What did the pancake say to the hungry preschooler? "Pick me up and roll me over."

* Follow the recipe for Fancy Sunday Morning Roll-Ups. When the pancake is finished and still warm, let the kids spoon 2 tablespoons vanilla or fruit-flavored yogurt over the pancake and top with their favorite preserve. Or, let them spread peanut butter and jelly over the pancake and roll it up jellyroll fashion to take wherever they want.

kids' caramel rolls and cinnamon twists

Who are we kidding here? These yummy rolls and twists are a favorite of adults, too, and they're a cinch to make—you can take it from me and my four-year-old sidekick, Dylan Paul. What makes them quick to fix is the store-bought bread-stick dough. What makes them delicious are the ingredients you put in the filling. No skimping here. By the way, the reason you get to choose between twists and rolls is Dylan. He didn't like all those "chewy things," so he took it upon himself to create the twists. Smart kid.

makes **6** twists and **6** rolls

¾ cup sugar, preferably superfine or baker's

1½ teaspoons ground cinnamon

⅓ cup toasted pecans (see note)

⅓ cup raisins or currants

¼ cup plus 1 tablespoon unsalted butter, melted

one 11-ounce tube refrigerated soft bread stick dough

* Preheat the oven to 375°F. Line a rimmed baking sheet with parchment paper or coat with nonstick spray, and set aside.

* In a small bowl, stir the sugar and cinnamon together. Divide the sugar mixture between two shallow bowls. To one bowl, add the pecans and raisins, and toss with the sugar mixture until coated. On a countertop, arrange in a row a shallow bowl filled with the melted butter, the bowl with the plain sugar-cinnamon mixture, and the bowl with the nut-and-raisin mixture.

to make twists:
Divide half the dough into 6 strips. Dip each dough strip into the butter, letting the excess drip back into the bowl. Lay each strip in the bowl with the plain sugar mixture, using your fingers to heavily sprinkle the mixture over the dough. Twist the dough into a spiral, and place it on the upper half of the prepared baking sheet. Leave a 1-inch space between each twist.

to make rolls:
Divide the remaining half of the dough into 6 strips. Dip each dough strip into the butter, letting the excess drip back into the bowl. Lay each strip in the nut-and-raisin mixture, using your fingers to heavily sprinkle the mixture over

the dough. Roll the dough into a spiral, making sure some of the nuts and raisins remain nestled within the spiraled dough. Insert a toothpick halfway into the side of the spiral to keep it from unraveling during baking. Place on the lower half of the prepared baking sheet, side by side, so the rolls are touching.

* Drizzle any remaining butter and sprinkle any of the remaining sugar mixtures over the rolls and twists before baking. Bake until lightly brown, 13 to 15 minutes. Transfer to a wire rack to cool. Remove the toothpicks from the rolls. Serve warm.

→ **note:**

To toast pecans, preheat the oven to 350°F. Spread the nuts on a rimmed baking sheet, and bake until lightly browned, 8 to 10 minutes.

sweet polenta muffins

These sunny yellow breakfast muffins are moist, tender, and irresistible. Whether they're served plain right from the oven or topped with warm fruit jam, one is never enough. Polenta is an Italian dish made from cornmeal. Avoid the coarsely cracked variety of cornmeal.

makes **12** muffins

1 ⅓ cups all-purpose flour

½ cup yellow cornmeal or polenta

½ cup sugar

1 teaspoon salt

1 tablespoon baking powder

½ cup (1 stick) unsalted butter, melted

⅔ cup milk

1 large egg

✳ Preheat the oven to 375°F. Coat twelve 2½-by-1½-inch muffin-pan cups with nonstick spray, and set aside.

✳ In a large bowl, whisk the flour, cornmeal, sugar, salt, and baking powder together until blended. In a small bowl, beat the melted butter, milk, and egg until well blended. Add the butter mixture to the flour mixture. Stir just until the flour is evenly moistened. Spoon the batter into the prepared muffin-pan cups.

✳ Bake until a toothpick inserted in the centers of the muffins comes out clean, 20 to 25 minutes. Remove immediately from pan. Transfer to a rack to cool slightly. Serve warm with warm fruit jam.

brie-scrambled eggs with ham

You can always count on scrambled eggs to be part of a tasty, nourishing breakfast or brunch. If brie isn't your family's favorite or your finicky eaters don't like "those little green things," leave out the herbs and substitute Jack or Cheddar cheese. For a festive drink, toast the day with a bubbly glass of Sunday Sippin'.

serves **4**

6 eggs

2 tablespoons water

pinch of salt

¼ pound brie cheese, at room temperature

2 tablespoons unsalted butter

¼ pound baked ham, cut into ½-inch squares

2 tablespoons chopped shallots

2 tablespoons chopped fresh parsley

¼ teaspoon dried tarragon leaves

✳ In a mixing bowl, lightly whisk the eggs, water, and salt so that a few streaks of white are still visible. Remove the cheese from the rind in small pieces, and set aside.

✳ In a well-seasoned, medium, heavy skillet over medium-low heat, melt the butter. As the foam subsides, sauté the ham and shallots for 2 minutes. Stir in the parsley and tarragon. Add the egg mixture to the same skillet and cook over medium heat, stirring slowly and steadily with a rubber spatula, until the eggs begin to soft-set, 1 to 1 ½ minutes. Add the cheese, and continue stirring slowly until the soft-set eggs hold their shape but are still creamy, about 1 minute. Serve immediately.

sunday sippin'

For super Sunday sipping, fill a fancy glass with ½ cup chilled ginger ale, ¼ cup chilled club soda, and a squeeze from an orange or lime wedge. For a sophisticated tang, add 2 drops Angostura bitters.

leaves of romaine chicken caesar salad

This is one of those caesar-style salads you'll find yourself using on many occasions. It makes a superb luncheon salad, a great dinner appetizer, and the perfect warm-weather weekend main meal. A few surprises give it crunch and flavor. And instead of using croutons, be sure to serve this salad with Pita Bread Parmesan Chips.

serves **4**

sunday night supper

dressing:

2 tablespoons freshly grated Parmigiano-Reggiano cheese

3 cloves garlic, minced

1 tablespoon Dijon mustard

2 tablespoons cider vinegar

¼ cup fresh lemon juice

¼ teaspoon Worcestershire sauce

1 cup mayonnaise

salt and freshly ground pepper

salad:

3 cups coarsely shredded cooked chicken

⅓ cup sweet midget pickles, rinsed and sliced

¼ cup capers, drained

1 head romaine lettuce, rinsed, dried, and torn into bite-sized pieces (8 cups)

Pita Bread Parmesan Chips (page 66)

to prepare the dressing:
In a 1-pint container with a tight-fitting lid, add the cheese, garlic, mustard, vinegar, lemon juice, Worcestershire sauce, and mayonnaise. Fasten the lid and shake until blended. Season with salt and pepper to taste. Set aside for 1 hour to blend flavors. (The dressing can be made ahead and refrigerated in a covered container for up to 5 days.)

to prepare the salad:
In a large salad bowl, combine the chicken, pickles, and capers. Add ⅓ cup dressing, and toss to coat. Marinate for 10 minutes. Add the romaine. Add and toss enough of the remaining dressing to coat the leaves. Taste, and season with salt and pepper. Garnish with the Pita Bread Parmesan Chips, and serve at once.

pita bread parmesan chips

These yummy chips taste great with salads. They taste great with soups. They also make delicious snacks and hors d'oeuvres.

makes **24** pieces

1 egg white, slightly beaten

2 tablespoons olive oil

2 teaspoons Dijon mustard

½ teaspoon minced garlic

½ teaspoon salt

¼ teaspoon dried dill

Pinch of freshly ground pepper

3 pita bread rounds, split in half horizontally

✳ Preheat the oven to 350°F. In a small bowl, whisk the egg white, oil, mustard, garlic, salt, dill, and pepper together until blended. Brush the cut surfaces of the pitas with the egg-white mixture, and cut each round into 8 wedges. On a baking sheet, place the wedges brushed-side up. Bake until crisp, about 25 minutes, reversing the baking sheet halfway through baking. Serve warm or at room temperature.

pasta bob

After an active weekend with kids, a supper with grown-up friends is a great way to celebrate. So, put on the pasta water, and let the kids have pasta with their favorite sauce from a jar and a room with a video. Now, get ready for one of the simplest, best, fine-dining pastas you'll ever taste. I promise. Oregon wine merchant Bob Liner created the dish years ago when he discovered the versatility of Cambozola cheese while working at an upscale delicatessen. The soft and creamy Bavarian cheese is a blue/brie hybrid made from milk with added cream. I think you'll find it sensational.

serves **4**

¼ pound (1 wedge) ripe Cambozola cheese, rind removed

1 pound dried fettuccine

¼ pound smoked Chinook salmon

½ cup (2 ounces) jarred roasted red pepper, drained and chopped in ½-inch dice

2 green onions, finely sliced

salt and pepper

∗ Warm the serving bowl or platter using hot water, drain, and dry. Add the cheese to the bowl in small pieces, and set aside.

∗ Meanwhile, cook the pasta according to package directions until al dente, which is tender but firm to the bite. Drain well, reserving ¼ cup cooking water in case you need it later.

∗ Immediately add the pasta to the serving bowl. Flake or crumble the salmon over the pasta. Add the peppers and green onions. Lightly toss to combine ingredients. For a moister coating, add 1 to 2 tablespoons reserved pasta water. Sprinkle with salt and pepper and serve immediately in warmed shallow bowls.

s'more sunday sundaes

No burning embers or campfire sticks are required for this ooey-gooey sundae. All you need are teddy bear grahams, some miniature marsh-mallows, and a reason to celebrate. (Forget tomorrow is Monday.)

makes **1** sundae

- 1 large marshmallow
- chocolate or confetti candy sprinkles for decorating
- 1 cup mini-marshmallows
- 1 scoop vanilla ice cream or frozen yogurt
- 1 scoop chocolate ice cream or frozen yogurt
- 2 to 3 tablespoons purchased chocolate or fudge sauce
- ⅓ cup teddy-bear-shaped graham cookies, broken graham crackers, or Golden Graham cereal

✳ Wipe the top of the large marshmallow with water, dip in sprinkles, and set aside. Turn on the broiler. Place the mini-marshmallows on a greased baking sheet or small ovenproof plate.

✳ Scoop the vanilla and chocolate ice cream into a dessert bowl and drizzle with the chocolate sauce.

✳ Cover with the cookies. Meanwhile, place the pan with the marshmallows under the broiler, watching carefully, until they just turn golden, 20 to 40 seconds. With a metal spatula, transfer to the top of the sundae. Top the sundae with the large marshmallow and serve immediately.

toys, crafts, and projects

smarty-pants apron

It's smart to put on an apron before starting a craft or following a recipe. This is a clever one your kids won't mind wearing a bit. With a little cutting and fabric paint, a pair of worn pants becomes a cool clothes-saver, complete with pockets. The trick? Cut off the pant legs and the whole front panel, then turn the pants around. The back panel becomes the apron's front, and the waistband takes the place of apron ties. Pretty neat.

for each apron you will need:

1 pair worn pants with two back pockets (see note)

scissors

tubes of fabric paint, with applicator tips

from start to finish

* On a flat work surface, lay the pants with the back pockets facing up. Using the scissors, cut off the pant legs, keeping the seat portion intact, 3 inches below the back pocket's lower edge. Following the side seams, cut up each side to the waistband. Using the waistband as a guide, cut off the pants' front panel, leaving the waistband (and top button) intact. Let your child use the fabric paints to decorate the apron with silly shapes and patterns. Let dry, and cure following the manufacturer's instructions.

→ **note:**

Choose pants with a front zipper that fit your child or ones that have a little extra room. Khakis or jeans outgrown by an older sibling work well.

incredibly cool clays

Here is a trio of homemade clays that are just right for little hands to squish, pat, mold, and press into fanciful shapes and sculptures for hours of weekend fun. It takes a grown-up hand to stir the stovetop mixtures, but the kids will have a great time choosing the colors and kneading the dough. Best of all, the resulting clays are soft and pliable, making them easy for even the youngest sculptors to mold into a masterpiece.

tools of the clay trade

Here's a list of useful tools straight from the kitchen cabinet:

comb, for making textured patterns

cookie-cutters and plastic candy molds, for making shapes

fork, for making textured patterns

garlic press, for making hair, grass, spaghetti, and creepy crawlies

knife (plastic or table), for cutting

rolling pin, for rolling and flattening clay

ruler, for marking or cutting straight lines

straws, for making holes

toothpicks, for making holes

play-do!

There's a reason this recipe is the hands-down favorite of parents and teachers everywhere. Kids love it. It's easy to clean up, and it keeps for a very long time.

makes about 1 ½ cups clay

2-quart saucepan

1 cup all-purpose flour

½ cup salt

2 teaspoons cream of tartar

1 cup water

1 teaspoon vegetable oil

5 to 6 drops food coloring, in desired color

* In the saucepan, combine the flour, salt, and cream of tartar. Stir in the water and oil. Over medium-low heat, stir the mixture constantly until it thickens and begins to form a ball, 3 to 5 minutes. Remove from heat.

* Turn the clay out onto a clean, protected surface. Let cool until it can be handled easily, about 3 minutes. Knead the clay until smooth. Add the food coloring to the clay, and knead until the color is evenly blended and the clay is smooth. The clay is ready to mold and shape. To store, wrap tightly in plastic wrap, and keep refrigerated for up to 6 weeks.

from start to finish

very best oven-baked clay

Hands-down, this is the very best of the oven-baked clays. When you want to make a lasting record of the weekend—and keep the kids happy at the same time—this is the clay for you. Easy to make and easy to use, it bakes to a smooth, hard finish that resembles the commercial varieties.

makes about **2** cups clay

2-quart saucepan

1 cup cornstarch, plus more for dusting

1 pound (16 ounces) box baking soda

1½ cups water

waxed paper

from start to finish

* In the saucepan, combine the cornstarch and baking soda. Stir in the water. Over medium-low heat, stir the mixture constantly until it thickens and begins to form a ball, 3 to 5 minutes. Remove from heat.

* Turn the clay out onto a surface lightly dusted with cornstarch. Let cool until it can be handled easily, about 3 minutes. Knead the clay until smooth. The clay is now ready to mold and shape. To store, wrap tightly in plastic wrap, and keep refrigerated for up to 3 weeks.

* Preheat the oven to 300°F. Line a baking sheet with waxed paper, and put the finished clay pieces on the prepared sheet. Bake for 30 minutes. Turn off the oven, leaving the tray and clay pieces in the oven for 1 more hour. Transfer to a wire rack to cool.

color-me-kool play dough

Calling all kids! The gang will cheer when the water is added and this playtime clay bursts with color and fragrance. Kool-Aid is the secret ingredient that gives this dough its vibrant color and fruity scent. The only question is what color and flavor to choose—wild cherry red, blueberry blue, or lemonade yellow. Better let the kids decide.

makes about **2** cups clay

2-quart saucepan

1 cup all-purpose flour

1 cup salt

1 tablespoon cream of tartar

1 package (0.13 ounces) unsweetened Kool-Aid, in desired color

1 cup warm water

1 tablespoon vegetable oil

* In the saucepan, combine the flour, salt, cream of tartar, and Kool-Aid. Stir in the water and oil. Over medium-low heat, stir the mixture constantly until it thickens and begins to form a ball, 3 to 5 minutes. Remove from the heat.

* Turn the clay out onto a clean, protected surface. Let cool until it can be handled easily, about 3 minutes. Knead the clay until smooth. The clay is ready to mold and shape. To store, wrap tightly in plastic wrap, and keep refrigerated for up to 3 weeks.

magnet-maze play board and place mat

Keep little ones busy until dinnertime by making and then playing with these clever magnet boards. Whether they draw a grand prix racetrack or a fairy-tale forest, their tiny toys will magically glide along the winding roads and scenery. It's all done with a magnet and paper clips. When it's time to eat, put the toys away, and use the play boards as place mats.

for each play board you will need:

> **craft glue**
>
> **1 paper clip**
>
> **1 tiny lightweight toy or paper cutout,
> such as a car, pony, or butterfly**
>
> **1 sheet construction paper or card stock**
>
> **felt-tipped pens, in assorted colors**
>
> **1 small refrigerator magnet**

* Using the craft glue, attach the paper clip to the underside of a selected toy or a paper cutout. Let dry. While the glue dries, lay the construction paper on a flat surface. Using the felt-tipped pens, decorate the play board with scenery as well as roads and paths for the toy to follow.

to play:
Hold the board in one hand, and place a toy on the finished surface, paper clip–side down. With your free hand, place a magnet directly under the toy and make the magnetic connection. Move the magnet around the board, making the toy travel across the board's surface.

milk paint

Early American settlers made milk paints in rich and creamy colors to paint their homes, barns, and fences. Here's a splashy version that's just right for weekend projects. The paint is shiny and paints a great picture, especially on heavier papers like construction paper and card stock.

makes 1 ¼ cups paint

one 14-ounce can sweetened condensed milk

5 cereal bowls

red, yellow, blue, and green food coloring

fork

5 empty glass jars with tight-fitting lids, such as baby food jars

from start to finish

* On a protected surface, measure and pour ¼ cup of the condensed milk into each bowl.

* Add 3 to 5 drops red food coloring to the first bowl. Add 3 to 5 drops yellow to the second. Add 3 to 5 drops blue to the third, and 3 to 5 drops green to the fourth. To make either orange or purple paint in the fifth bowl, add 3 to 5 drops of red and yellow, or 3 to 5 drops of red and blue. For pastel colors, add 1 or 2 drops less coloring. For more vivid colors, add 1 or 2 drops more coloring.

* Starting with the first bowl, use the fork to mix the food coloring into the milk, stirring until the color is blended. Rinse the fork, and repeat with each color. Pour the paints into jars for painting and storage. The paint will keep tightly sealed and refrigerated for up to 3 weeks.

quick-clip weekend journal

Turn a stack of your family's best drawings, weekend notes, or postcards from a road trip into a book of lasting memories with this quick-clip technique. To make any size book you wish, follow these instructions, adjusting the size of the paper and the binder clips.

for each journal you will need:

papers for binding

assorted stickers

felt-tipped pens, in assorted colors

2 sheets card stock or construction paper, the same size as the papers for binding

three 1-inch binder clips

✳ Collect and organize the papers you wish to bind in a neat stack, and set aside. To make the journal's front cover, using the stickers and felt-tipped pens decorate 1 sheet of card stock. (The date and your children's signatures can be added to the back cover where a logo would appear.)

✳ To assemble the journal, add the front and back covers to the collected papers, making sure the edges are evenly matched. Attach the binder clips to the journal's left-hand edge, with the first clip about 1 inch from the journal's top edge and the second about 1 inch from the bottom edge. Place the third clip halfway between the two. Flip the wire tabs into place, closing the clips. With the clips closed, remove the wire tab from each side of the clips.

chalk-it-up pet place mat

Just like people place mats, these mats keep crumbs in check so your four-legged family members can munch and crunch without messy cleanup for you. A can of chalkboard spray paint, a plastic place mat, and a box of chalk are the ingredients for this quick-as-a-weekend project—and your pet can use the resulting masterpiece all week long.

makes **1** place mat

newspaper

one 12-ounce can green or black chalkboard spray paint

1 plastic place mat, with smooth surface

white or colored chalk with calcium carbonate, such as Crayola brand

clear acrylic spray

✳ In a well-ventilated area, protect a flat surface with several layers of newspaper. Following the directions on the can of spray paint, apply a light, even coat to the place mat's top surface and sides. Let dry, about 15 minutes. Turn the mat over to paint the other side. Repeat the process to apply 2 more coats. Set aside to cure for 24 hours.

✳ Using the chalk, decorate the place mat's chalkboard surface with pet-friendly art. To make the chalk designs permanent, seal with 2 light coats of acrylic spray, making sure to hold the can at least 14 inches from the decorated surface, otherwise the design will blur.

chalk-it-up travel mat

Heading out of town for the weekend or the park for a picnic? This chalkboard mat and a box of chalk will keep kids busy for hours. Thin, lightweight, and durable, the mat slips easily into a suitcase or backpack, just right for getaway weekends and holiday trips.

✳ Follow the recipe for Chalk-It-Up Pet Place Mat, omitting the permanent design and sealing steps. When the chalkboard paint is dry, season the surface by rubbing the side of a white chalk piece over the whole mat. Wipe the mat clean with a chalk eraser.

Is your cat purr-fect? Is your dog the most devoted of pals? Then it's time to reward them with their own special dishes for weekend meals. Oven-cured porcelain paint makes it possible to dress up a classic ceramic pet dish with nothing more than a rubber stamp and a little imagination. Best of all, because the paint doesn't become permanent until after it's baked, you can wipe mistakes away. When the bowl is done, fill it with an extra-nice treat. Meow, woof-woof!

makes **1** bowl

1 ceramic pet dish, with a smooth surface (see note)

hot water

distilled white vinegar

1 porcelain-paint felt-tipped pen, in desired color (see note)

1-or 2-inch rubber stamp, in desired pattern

cotton swabs

kitchen scrub brush

cont'd...

✳ Clean the pet dish with hot water and vinegar. Let dry, and set aside.

✳ Set the bowl and your decorating materials on a protected surface. Using the pen, apply an even coat of paint to the rubber stamp's raised design, following the manufacturer's instructions. Place the coated stamp over the dish where you want the design to appear. Press the stamp firmly onto the dish's surface. To keep the design from smearing, carefully lift the stamp straight up. If the ink doesn't stamp evenly, use the pen to touch up the design. Add your own freehand patterns and borders to complement the stamped design or personalize the dish with your pet's name. Using moist cotton swabs, remove any smears or bits of stray paint as you work. When stamping is complete, clean the rubber stamp with soapy water and a scrub brush. Allow the dish to cure for 24 hours.

✳ Preheat the oven to 325°F. Put the cured dish directly on the oven rack, and bake for 35 minutes. Transfer to a wire rack to cool.

→ **note:**

Ceramic pet dishes are available where pet supplies are sold.

✳ Porcelain-paint felt-tipped pens (such as Porcelaine 150) are available at art-supply and craft stores. If the manufacturer's curing or baking times differ from those listed here, follow their recommendations.

variation:

If you find the perfect pet bowl with a raised design, using the porcelain paint pen, outline and enhance the design. (See photo "Good Dog" pet bowl.)

five-minute fun-in-the-tub toys

A few around-the-house supplies and the five minutes it takes to fill the bathtub are all you need to make a water toy that's not only safe but is guaranteed to be a splish-splashing success. Whether you make one or all of the following tub-time treats, your kids will end up staying in the tub to paint, pour, and play until the water goes bye-bye.

bath-time finger paints

Make bath time a great time with a batch of these squeaky-clean finger paints that you whip up while the bathtub fills. A can of shaving cream and a few drops of food coloring make a colorful foam kids can use to paint on the tub, the tile, and their own sweet selves. When it's time to get out of the tub, the paints simply wash away, leaving both bathtub and kids clean as a whistle.

for each set of finger paints you will need:

1 can shaving cream

4 pint-sized plastic containers

red, yellow, blue, and green food coloring

fork

❋ Put 1 cup shaving cream into each container. Add 4 to 5 drops red food coloring to the first bowl, 4 to 5 drops yellow to the second bowl, 4 to 5 drops blue to the third bowl, and 4 to 5 drops green to the fourth bowl. For pastel colors, add 1 or 2 drops less coloring. For more vivid colors, add 1 or 2 drops more coloring. Starting with the first bowl, use the fork to mix the food coloring into the foam, stirring until the color is blended. Rinse the fork, and repeat with each color.

funny-face funnel

Let the good times pour all the way through bath-time with this funny-face funnel. It takes just a minute to make. You cut a plastic milk jug in half to create the funnel and let your little bathing buddies add the funny face. Pssst: Hair washing is a breeze when the rinse water pours through this funnel's silly snout.

for each funnel you will need:

empty 1-gallon plastic milk jug with lid

felt-tipped permanent markers, in assorted colors

scissors

✳ Place the gallon jug on its side. Using a marker, draw a line around the jug about 1 inch below its handle. Using the scissors, pierce the jug on the marked line. Then, using the hole as an opening, cut along the marked guideline to remove the jug's base.

✳ Starting with the pour spout for a nose, use the markers to give the funnel its funny face. Add the eyes, ears, and mouth, along with other funny features like a silly hat, or a polka dot tie.

"whose big toe is that?"

Get a close look at what's under the water with this homemade magnifier you can make in a wink with a plastic soda bottle and plastic wrap. The water's pressure, pushing against the plastic wrap, creates the concave magnifying lens—even a baby sister's tiny toe will look really big.

for each magnifier you will need:

empty 1-liter clear plastic bottle

felt-tipped permanent marker

scissors

plastic wrap

3-inch rubber band

✳ Place the bottle on its side. Using the marker, draw a line around the bottle 3 inches below the top opening. Repeat to mark 3 inches from its base. Using the scissors, pierce the bottle on the top marked line. Using the hole as an opening, cut along the marked line to remove the bottle's top section. Repeat to remove the lower section. Cover 1 end of the cylinder with plastic wrap, using the rubber band to hold the wrap in place.

under-the-covers flashlight

Hey, kids, the lights are out. Everyone's in bed. Pull the covers over your head, and switch on this super-cool flashlight. Let the fun begin!

for each flashlight you will need:

stickers, in favorite theme

small flashlight

4 or 5 lightweight plastic toys, each 2 to 3 inches long

glue gun and hot glue sticks (see note)

skip to my room

* Select the stickers and place them on the flashlight, being careful not to cover the battery compartment. Arrange the toys where you wish them to appear on the flashlight's side panels. (Make sure the flashlight can still be held easily.) Using the glue gun, attach each toy with a generous stream of hot glue. Let dry, 15 to 20 seconds.

→ **note:**

A hot glue gun is recommended because it bonds firmly and dries quickly. Glue guns should always be used with care and only by adults. If you don't have a glue gun, or little fingers are tackling this project, craft glue can be substituted. Craft glue takes longer to dry, so the toys must be held in place while they set.

things to do with a flashlight in the dark

1 Be a between-the-sheets explorer.

2 Read a book.

3 Play flashlight tag.

4 Make hand shadows and shapes on the wall.

5 Make light patterns on the wall. Using a toothpick, poke a series of holes in a pattern on the bottom of a small paper cup. Shine the flashlight into the cup.

6 Point the flashlight straight up under your chin so that the light shines and casts shadows on your face, and tell a spooky story.

7 Check for wild things under the bed and in the closet.

can-do-it desk organizer

Kids will love keeping their pencils, crayons, scissors, and other important desktop tools in this handy "I made it myself" desk organizer.

for each desk organizer you will need:

3 empty cans, in different sizes

2 large 4-inch rubber bands

scissors

white self-adhesive vinyl shelf paper

stickers

felt-tipped pens, in assorted colors

* Arrange the cans in a tight group, with sides touching. Hold the cans in place by placing 1 rubber band around the arrangement 1 inch from the shortest can's top rim and a second rubber band 1 inch from the cans' bottom edges.

* Using the scissors, cut a strip of vinyl shelf paper 2 to 3 inches wide and long enough to wrap all the way around the grouped cans. Let your child decorate the strip with the stickers and felt-tipped pens.

* Peel the shelf paper's adhesive backing. Holding the grouped cans in one hand, use your free hand to position the strip between the rubber bands at the cans' midsection. Wrap the strip around the cans and smooth into place. Remove the rubber bands, and the organizer is ready to use.

skip to my room

secret message tube and doorknob hanger

Every kid knows that secret messages are a cool way to communicate. Indulge the secret agents in your house with their own message tubes that do double duty as nameplates on bedroom doorknobs. All it takes are paper-towel tubes camouflaged with bright paper, colorful ribbons, and some cryptic correspondence.

for each hanger you will need:

scissors

9-by-12-inch construction-paper sheet, in a favorite color

1 cardboard paper-towel tube

clear adhesive tape

1-inch decorative adhesive letters

paper punch

8 lengths curly ribbon, in assorted colors, each 36 inches (1 yard) long

54-inch (1½ yard length) ⅞-inch satin or grosgrain ribbon, in a favorite color

* Using the scissors, trim the construction paper so that its length matches the length of the paper-towel tube. Wrap the construction paper around the tube, and secure it with the tape. Using the adhesive letters, add a name or message to the wrapped tube's surface, opposite the paper's taped edge.

* Using the paper punch, punch 4 holes around each of the tube's opening edges. Thread 1 curly ribbon through 1 hole, about 3 inches. Tie in a tight double knot so that the knot is touching the tube. Repeat with the remaining ribbon lengths.

* Thread the satin ribbon all the way through the tube. Holding a ribbon end in each hand, bring the ends together over the tube's center point. Tie a knot for hanging about 9 inches from the ribbon ends, and finish with a bow. Hang on a bedroom door, ready to receive messages.

tasty tweets

With an orange, some twine, and a little help from the kitchen cabinet, you and your little flock can make this adorable feeder with its dangling orange-rind cutouts. You cut the orange and scrape out the fruit, while your kids mix the bird-friendly filling. You use a citrus zester to decorate the feeder cup with swirls and curls, while the kids use tiny cookie- or garnish-cutters to cut shapes from the remaining rind. Even though the feeder takes less than an hour to make, it may take a few days for this hanging tweet to be discovered. Don't worry, soon you'll have a flock of hungry guests.

makes 1 feeder

½ cup chunky peanut butter

½ cup birdseed

sharp 7-inch knife

1 large navel orange

spoon

1-inch cookie- or garnish-cutter,
    in desired shape

wooden skewer

citrus zester (see note)

8 lengths natural twine or raffia,
    each 36 inches (1 yard) long

cont'd...

to make the filling:

In a large bowl, mix the peanut butter and birdseed together until well blended. The mixture should hold together without being too sticky. Set aside.

to make the feeder:

Using the sharp knife, cut the orange in half. Using the spoon, carefully scoop out the fruit from each half. Gently scrape each rind clean, making sure not to tear the peel. Set 1 orange-rind half aside.

✳ On a protected surface, cut or tear the other half of the orange rind into 2 or 3 sections. With the rind-side down, begin at the outside edge of each section, and press the cutter all the way through the peel. Remove the cutout shape, and continue to cut out as many different shapes as the rind allows. One orange half yields 3 to 5 cutouts. To make holes for hanging the cutouts, using the wooden skewer, puncture a hole at the top of each cutout. Set aside.

✳ In one hand, hold the remaining orange-rind half. With the other hand, using the citrus zester at an angle, press a single hole firmly against the peel. Applying constant pressure, pull the zester across the fruit, scoring the rind in simple stripes and spirals.

✳ Using the skewer, puncture 4 holes, ½ inch from the rim, at each quarter point around the orange. Next, tie a double knot at the end of a length of twine. Trim the knotted end to ¼ inch. Thread the twine's unknotted end through 1 of the holes, from the inside to the outside. String an orange cutout onto the twine. Place it where you wish it to appear on the twine, and secure it in place with a knot. Repeat to add the remaining twine lengths and cutouts.

to assemble the feeder:

Spoon the filling into the prepared orange-rind half, mounding the mixture just past the rim. Gather the 4 lengths of twine. At about the 12-inch point, tie the twine with a double knot. Leave the remaining lengths for hanging.

→ **note:**

Citrus zesters are available at specialty kitchen stores. Look for one that has a row of 5 tiny holes.

birdie bistro

You and your kids aren't the only ones who enjoy a nice meal out on the weekend. What about your feathered friends and those swift-winged tourists flying through your backyard in search of a good feast?

Here's a bird feeder you and the kids can start in the morning and have open for business by lunch. After the kids fill it with birdseed appetizers or swell suet suppers, stand back and wait for those four-star chirps and twitters.

makes **1** feeder

ruler

black felt-tipped pen

½-gallon dairy carton, empty, clean, and dry

scissors

glue gun and hot glue sticks

spring-style clothespin

flat-edged paintbrush, ½ inch wide

one 8-ounce bottle gesso (see note)

one 2-ounce bottle acrylic paint or ½ cup Milk Paint (page 80), in desired color

assorted stickers (optional)

felt-tipped pens, in assorted colors (optional)

clear acrylic spray

paper punch

40 paper clips

cont'd...

* Using the ruler and pen, measure and draw a line around the carton 2 inches from its base. Repeat to draw a line around the carton's top section, 1 ¼ inches from the point where the carton's body and slanted top meet.

* Using the scissors, pierce the carton just above the 2-inch base line. Using the hole as an opening, carefully cut out the carton's base, following the marked guideline. Next, using the marked guidelines, cut out the carton's slanted top piece. Discard the center section.

* To seal the top section of the carton, open the carton's flaps halfway so that the two outside flaps are open and the pouring spout is folded closed. Using the glue gun, apply a stream of hot glue along the flaps where the carton was originally sealed. Close the flaps, and secure with the clothespin until the glue is dry, about 30 seconds.

* On a protected surface, using the paintbrush, cover the outside surface of both carton sections with a generous coat of gesso, making sure all lettering and logos are concealed. Let dry, 30 to 40 minutes. Using the cleaned brush, apply an even coat of paint to the outside surface of both carton sections and let dry, about 1 hour for acrylic paint and overnight for Milk Paint.

* If necessary, apply a second coat. If desired, decorate the painted sections using stickers and felt-tipped pens. Seal the finished carton with 2 or 3 light coats of acrylic spray.

* Using the paper punch, punch a hole through the upper section's side panel, next to 1 corner, about 1/4 inch from the cut edge. Punch a second hole on the opposite side panel, directly across from the first hole. Punch 2 more parallel holes at the other end of the panel. Repeat to match and punch 2 sets of corresponding holes in the base section's side panels.

* To connect the carton sections and assemble the bird feeder, string 5 paper clips into a chain. Repeat to make 3 more paper clip chains. Set the remaining paper clips aside.

* Attach the last paper clip in 1 chain to a hole in the upper roof section. Attach the other end of the chain to the corresponding hole in the lower feeder section. Repeat to attach the 3 remaining chains to the roof and feeder sections.

* To hang the feeder, punch a hole in the feeder's roof at its center point. String the remaining 20 paper clips into a chain, and attach it to the roof's hole, ready to hang.

If gesso is unavailable, paint the bird feeder using acrylic paint, adding 1 or 2 drops dishwashing liquid to help the paint adhere to the carton's waxy surface. If necessary, add an extra coat of paint to cover lettering and logos. If you're using Milk Paint, you'll need the gesso.

neat tweet carton (or bow-wow box)

* Keep birdseed ready and waiting in this clever carton that kids can make to match their Birdie Bistro. To paint and decorate a clean quart-size carton, follow the recipe for Birdie Bistro, omitting the measuring, cutting, and hanging steps.

* For a Bow-Wow Box, paint and decorate the carton following the recipe for Chalk-It-Up Pet Place Mat (page 84).

flights-of-fancy dress-up suitcase

Weekend trips to the land of make-believe are lots more fun when the costumes, dress-up clothes, and glitzy accessories are all in one handy place. You and your fantasy travelers can begin by transforming an old suitcase or plastic bin into a trunk of dreams with stickers, glitter glue, and imagination.

makes **1** dress-up suitcase

assorted stickers

**1 old suitcase not made from cloth, clean,
with working clasps**

self-adhesive vinyl letters

glitter glue, in assorted colors

assorted clothes, costumes, and accessories

✳ On a protected surface, using the stickers, decorate 1 side of the suitcase. Using letters, spell out names or words such as "bon voyage." Apply the glitter glue in a thin stream to outline the stickers and letters. You also can add patterns and designs. Let dry, about 24 hours. Turn the suitcase over, and decorate the remaining side.

✳ Fill the suitcase with assorted clothes, costumes, and accessories, such as frilly petticoats, fancy dresses, old suits, workman's coveralls, lab jackets, aprons (you get the idea), as well as a variety of hats, wigs, eyeglasses, and costume jewelry.

glowing star magic case

Young magicians will love to store the mysterious tools of their trade in this glow-in-the-dark case. Follow the directions for a Flights-of-Fancy Dress-Up Suitcase, using a vanity-style case. Proceed as directed, substituting self-adhesive glow-in-the-dark stars for the stickers. For a magical effect, finish the case with a light coat of silver or gold glitter spray.

bouncing-ball piggy bank

Kids will love dropping their change into this roly-poly bank that they can make faster than a little piggy can go to market. Buy a few inexpensive balls on Friday for a weekend of rolling, tossing, and bouncing. Then, when the kids want something to do, right away, gather up the balls and the supplies to make a whole barnyard full of thrifty pigs. It's a good idea to have the kids practice where they want the legs, tail, and face to go before you attach the pieces with glue. For more fun features, use a felt-tipped pen to add eyelashes or a piggly-wiggly smile.

makes **1** piggy bank

cutting board

1 hollow bouncing ball, with a 5-to-6-inch
    circumference

craft knife

glue gun and hot glue sticks (see note)

4 matching corks, each ½ to ¾ inch long

1 pipe cleaner, in desired color,
    cut into a 5-inch length

pencil

small wiggle eyes or small matching buttons
    and beads (see safety note)

one ½-inch button

scissors

two 3-by-3-inch felt squares, in desired colors

cont'd...

✳ On the cutting board, place the ball so that the seam is circling the ball horizontally. To make the piggy bank's coin slot, hold the ball firmly in place with one hand. Using the craft knife, cut a 1½-inch slit all of the way through the ball's surface casing.

✳ On a protected surface, place the ball, slot-side down. To add the piggy bank's legs, using the glue gun, apply a generous dot of glue to a cork's larger end, and lightly press it on the bank. Hold it in place until the glue sets, 10 to 15 seconds. Repeat to add the remaining 3 corks.

✳ To curl the pig's tail, wrap the pipe cleaner around a pencil, leaving 1 inch at the end straight. Using the craft knife, pierce a small hole in the bank where you wish the tail to be. Insert the tail's uncurled portion into the hole.

✳ To add the face, attach the eyes and button snout with dots of glue. Using the scissors, cut small, pointed ears from the felt squares. Glue the ears on the top of the head, above the eyes and forehead.

→ **note:**
A hot glue gun is recommended because it bonds firmly and dries quickly. Glue guns should always be used with care and only by adults. If you don't have a glue gun, or little fingers are tackling this project, craft glue can be substituted. Craft glue takes longer to dry, so the pig's features must be held in place while they set.

→ **safety note:**
Wiggle eyes and buttons can be a choking hazard for children under 5. Use caution, and supervise.

piggy-perfect pencil holder
Follow the recipe for Bouncing-Ball Piggy Bank to create this handy desk accessory. Proceed as directed, replacing the coin slot with 4 or 5 small pencil-sized slits. To store a pencil, push it into a slit.

yippee-yi yo-yo

Everyone will love "walking the dog," "rocking the baby," and "shooting the moon" with this flashy orb. A plain wooden yo-yo becomes a sparkling satellite when it's coated with bright paint, glitter, and beads.

makes **1** yo-yo

> **paintbrush**
>
> **acrylic paint, in your favorite color**
>
> **wooden or plastic yo-yo**
>
> **tiny beads or sequins**
>
> **metallic glitter**
>
> **white glue**

* On a protected surface, using the paintbrush and acrylic paint, cover 1 side of the yo-yo, and let dry. (Don't paint the inside edge near the string.) Turn the yo-yo over, paint the other side, and let dry.

* In a saucer, mix the beads and glitter together. Using the cleaned paintbrush, apply the glue to the yo-yo's flat surface on 1 side. Dip the glued surface into the bead-and-glitter mixture. Tap off the excess beads and glitter, and repeat on the other side. Let dry.

funny-paper bingo

After you've had your chance at the morning paper, give the funny papers to the kids. In less time than it takes you to brew your coffee, they can turn comic strips into a bingo game the whole family will love.

makes **1** game

sunday funny papers

scissors

glue stick

1 paper lunch sack

3 or 4 sheets construction paper,
    in assorted colors

playing tokens, 10 to 12 for each player
    (see safety note)

to make the game:

From the Sunday funny papers, select a comic strip for each player. Choose comic strips that all have the same number of frames and are not on back-to-back pages. Using the scissors, carefully cut out a strip, following its outside edge. Repeat to cut out the remaining strips. These become the playing cards.

to decorate the game sack:

Using the glue stick, adhere the logo for the entire comics section, along with cutouts from the remaining comic strips, to the lunch sack. Set aside and let dry, 5 to 10 minutes.

✳ Count the total number of frames in all the comic-strip playing cards, then double the number. (For example, 4 comic strips, each with 6 frames, would total 24 frames. When doubled, the final total would be 48.) This will be the number of bingo word cards you will need. Cut the construction paper into the number of 2-by-3-inch cards needed.

✳ Select a number of frequently used words, such as, "now," "the," "what," "how," and "maybe," along with a variety of words appearing in the comic-strip playing cards. Write 1 word on each card. If the strips include frames without words, leave several cards blank. Place the finished cards in the decorated sack.

to play the game:
Give each player a comic-strip playing card and a handful of tokens. Place the word cards in the decorated sack. Beginning with the youngest player, have the player draw a card and read the word out loud. Players with that word on one of their frames mark the frame with a token. Players take turns drawing and calling out words until a player fills each frame of his or her strip and calls, "Bingo!"

toys and games

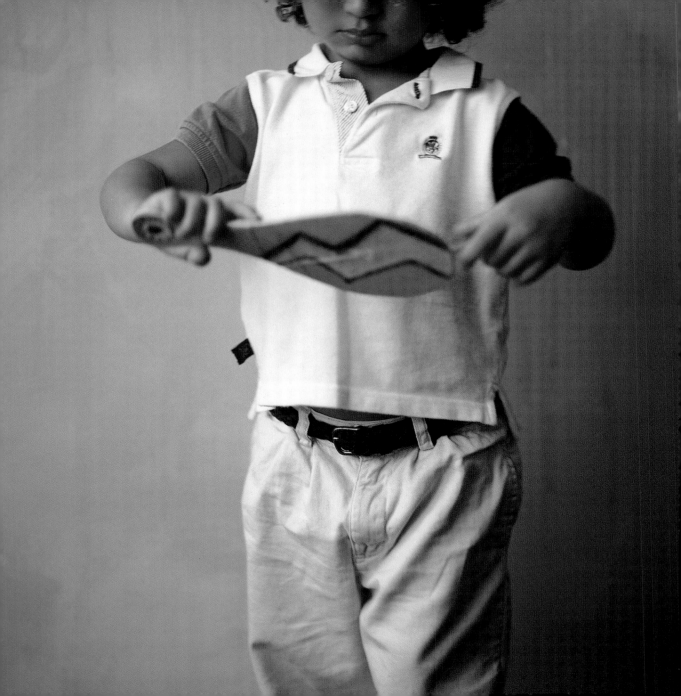

whop-'em, bop-'em paddle balls

With a paintbrush, brightly colored paints, and a sticker or two, you and your kids can give a paddle ball a whoppin' make-over, and give the family a whop-'em, bop-'em great time. Kids can play solo or team up to see who can paddle the longest, with a "no chores today" prize for the winner and sweet snacks for every runner-up. (Check out that yummy Snicker-Snack Granola, page 28.)

makes **1** paddle ball

> paintbrush
>
> acrylic paint, in your favorite color
>
> paddle ball
>
> fabric paints, with applicator tips
>
> assorted stickers

* On a protected surface, using the paintbrush and acrylic paint, cover 1 side of the paddle. Let the paint dry. Turn the paddle over, and paint the other side. When the paint is dry, using the fabric paints, add simple decorative patterns, such as polka dots or stripes. You also can decorate the painted paddle with stickers.

weekend activities and outings

In this chapter, you'll find interesting, engaging, and loving ways
to be with your family. Snappy ideas for family activities, games,
projects, and crafts will keep everyone absorbed.
Suggestions for snacks and treats make it all much more fun.
Here, too, are helpful hints for those in-between times when
there's so much to do that there's nothing to do, or when we want
to spend a little time by ourselves.

game night

No homework, no meetings, no get-ready-for-school night. When the evening is young, gather the gang for some friendly competition and mighty-fine snacking. Round up their favorite board games, go one-to-one on the Candy Land trail, or set out on an "I Spy" adventure. Team up to play a game of charades, hide-and-seek, or a 'round-the-house scavenger hunt. See what games the kids can make up on their own. All it takes is a few simple ideas to get them started. Big-bottle bowling made with empty plastic soda bottles and a foam ball is both fun and easy. So is playing with food. Save some of that snacking popcorn, load a piece of popcorn in a plastic spoon, and flick it into an empty egg carton. (Make up point values for the different cups.) Complete the evening by serving your in-house competitors a game-time snack and something frosty to drink.

kids can use the following craft projects in games while enjoying these refreshments:

crafts

yippee-yi yo-yo (page 102)

whop-'em, bop-'em paddle balls (page 107)

funny-paper bingo (page 104)

bouncing-ball piggy bank (page 99)

recipes

hairy pepper and the green goblet (page 12)

sweet finger salad with romaine and mint (page 15)

flavored-sugar popcorn (page 22)

banana-rama-ding-dongs (page 46)

everybody's favorite everything cookie (page 31)

kaleidoscope kooler (page 36)

no-more-homework chocolate soda (page 35)

dinner party at the family restaurant

Who says you have to go out? Turn your family dining room into a fancy restaurant, a neighborhood cafe, or a let-the-play-begin supper club. Kids design the menus, dress up like waiters, and act the parts of sous-chef or pastry cook. They can decorate the table according to the theme of the dinner, set votive candles at each place setting, create a fancy-folded napkin, and, for fun, paint or decorate a sign with the name of your restaurant. When dessert is over, propose a toast, and let the entertainment begin. Perhaps it's a talent show, a dress-up play, or a karaoke sing-along. Whatever happens, it will be a great night on the town.

you can include these craft projects and recipes:

crafts

magnet-maze play board and place mat (page 79)

chalk-it-up travel mat (page 84)

flights-of-fancy dress-up suitcase (page 98)

glowing star magic case (page 98)

recipes

mighty-fine meat loaf with barbecue sauce (page 50)

make mine mashed potatoes (page 52)

leaves of romaine chicken caesar salad (page 65)

pita bread parmesan chips (page 66)

fancy-fingers coconut and ice-cream cake (page 54)

s'more sunday sundaes (page 69)

make it fun, make it a gift

There's something special about sitting around a table and making crafts together. It's a time to visit with kids and a chance to share creativity. Doing crafts with kids makes for life-long memories, and in the process develops their problem-solving skills and confidence. Let those special times do double duty by encouraging your kids to make presents for others. Grandparents, moms and dads, school friends, and neighbors will treasure their gifts. To keep creative juices flowing, make sure to have plenty of snacks and liquid refreshments on hand.

you can include these craft projects and recipes:

crafts

can-do-it desk organizer (page 91)

bouncing-ball piggy bank (page 99)

piggy-perfect pencil holder (page 101)

quick-clip weekend journal (page 83)

under-the-covers flashlight (page 90)

yippee-yi yo-yo (page 102)

whop-'em, bop-'em paddle balls (page 107)

recipes

hairy pepper and the green goblet (page 12)

"quick! i'm hungry" sandwich ideas (page 20)

seasoned-in-a snap popcorn (page 22)

frozen lollipop fruit swirls (page 45)

crazy-crust pizza (page 40)

"quick! i'm thirsty" drink ideas (page 36)

on the patio, in the yard, or at the park

There's a world of outdoor fun just outside the front door waiting for you and your family. Dress for the weather and head out for some fresh air and exercise. Catch the wind with a kite, or capture one another with a game of freeze tag. Take along the sidewalk chalk for impromptu drawings or ABC hopscotch. Food tastes better when it's eaten outside, so pack up portable snacks and beverages.

you may want to take along these crafts and treats:

weekend activities
and outings

waterworks

Kids love water, anytime, anyplace. In the house, a warm, sudsy bath is a great way to clean up at the end of a busy Saturday, and it's also a fun place to have an indoor recess. (So is the kitchen sink, standing on a step-up stool.) Outdoors, there's the yard pool to keep kids in the swim. There's also that nearby lake, the river, or a sandy beach with tide pools and shallow inlets. Whether it's staying cool in the summer sun or soaking in the tub, kids will love it even more with a few simple toys they've helped to make. When your water babies are clean and dry, give them each his or her own lunch packed in a plastic beach pail, or surprise the squeaky-clean set with an after-bath treat.

consider including these crafts and snacks:

pets on a pedestal

Whether they meow, bark, chatter, or chirp, your pets are members of your family, and they're just as happy as you are that it's the weekend. They know the signals: no alarm clock, no schoolbooks, no running for the bus.
Just lazy mornings, a hop on the bed, a scratch on the head, and maybe a game of fetch. You and the kids can show your pets—and the feathered friends who live in your neighborhood—how much they are loved by making it a pet-on-a-pedestal day. With these pet-pleasing projects and tasty treats, it's easy to give them the V.I.P. (very important pet) treatment.

here are a few treats for your animal allies:

crafts

chalk-it-up pet place mat (page 84)

**get-out-the-good-china pet bowl
(page 85)**

**neat tweet carton (or a bow-wow box)
(page 97)**

tasty tweets (page 93)

birdie bistro (page 95)

let's plan some fun

Who wants to sleep in a bed anyway, especially when it's the weekend and you can have a slumber-party camp-out in the family room or on the porch or patio? Make sure there's enough room for the whole gang to roll out sleeping bags. (Remove any breakable stuff in the area first.) Turn a lamp into a night light with a low-voltage bulb, or string holiday lights around the door. When it's time for a midnight munchie, turn on your flashlights and tiptoe to the kitchen for some super snacks. Then snuggle up side-by-side and whisper a few ghost stories, or watch a scary movie.

these crafts and snacks are perfect for camp-outs:

crafts

under-the-covers flashlight (page 90)

quick-clip weekend journal (page 83)

flights-of-fancy dress-up suitcase (page 98)

funny-paper bingo (page 104)

whop-'em, bop-'em paddle balls (page 107)

recipes

crazy-crust pizza (page 40)

sweet finger salad with romaine and mint (page 15)

seasoned-in-a-snap popcorn (page 22)

rocky-road marshmallow crispies (page 25)

everybody's favorite everything cookie (page 31)

good-for-you float (page 36)

weekend bubbly (page 36)

sleep-in sundays

Between you and me, sleeping in on Sunday morning is a little like winning the lottery. Everyone dreams of it, but few win the prize, especially with a houseful of active kids. One way to increase the odds of some extra shut-eye—or some uninterrupted time with the Sunday paper—is to keep the kids busy amusing themselves. All it takes are a few simple preparations on Saturday night. To ease early-morning hunger pangs, arrange a tray of ready-to-fix or already prepared breakfast snacks on the kitchen counter. To keep busy fingers and minds happy, cover the family-room table with a protective cloth, and set out games and art supplies for a morning's worth of kid-friendly activities. And, last but not least, there's always a favorite movie that's rewound and ready to play.

here are some games, activities, and food ideas for a blissful Sunday:

crafts

incredibly cool clays (page 74)

funny-paper bingo (page 104)

magnet-maze play board and place mat
   (page 79)

chalk-it-up travel mat (page 84)

recipes

muffin à la mode (page 49)

frozen lollipop fruit swirls (page 45)

dippity-do frosted fruit tray (page 49)

on-the-go waffle cone (page 49)

bowl-me-over (page 49)

kids' caramel rolls and cinnamon twists
   (page 60)

creamy-dreamy orange smoothie (page 36)

weekend activities
and outings

"what can I do now?"

weekend activities and outings

by myself

1 Place a sheet of paper on a table in front of a mirror. Looking into the mirror, draw a picture or self-portrait. Tricky, isn't it?

2 Make an alphabet book. Write each letter of the alphabet on a sheet of plain paper. Then draw a picture of someone or something whose name starts with that letter.

3 Build a couch-cushion castle on the family-room floor.

4 Read aloud.

5 Make a bookmark. Cut pictures from used greeting cards and glue them onto the front and back of a construction-paper strip.

6 Draw faces on your fingers using washable felt-tipped pens. Put on a 10-finger puppet show.

7 Make thumbprint creatures by pressing your thumb onto a stamp pad, then firmly pressing the thumb onto a blank sheet of paper. (Clean the ink off your thumb by pressing it onto a wet paper towel.) Now add little arms, legs, antennae, and tails to the thumbprint with a pencil or washable felt-tipped pen.

8 Make a paper-bag puppet or a cool cootie-catcher using felt-tipped markers and stickers.

9 Call a friend on the telephone.

10 Write to a pen pal.

when it's raining

11 Capture rain in a jar, and measure how much you caught with a ruler.

12 Eat a picnic lunch, complete with picnic blanket, on the family-room floor.

13 Play Lava Land. Take the cushions off the sofa and the chairs. Lay them on the floor within jumping distance. Pretend the ground is hot lava and the cushions are cool, safe land. (Before getting started, better check with the grown-ups.)

14 Dance in the rain.

15 Make a paperweight. Using acrylic paint and a small paintbrush, paint a picture on a smooth stone.

16 Go on a puddle walk in your raincoat, hat, and boots.

17 Have an adult mix a few drops of food coloring into some dishwashing liquid, and paint pictures on the windowpanes.

18 Decorate a week's supply of brown-paper lunch bags with felt-tipped pens, crayons, and stickers.

19 Create your own bookplates by decorating plain self-adhesive labels with felt-tipped pens and stickers. (Don't forget your name.)

20 Fill a mixing bowl with dried beans. Collect 5 to 10 small objects (avoiding those with sharp edges), such as a gumdrop, a key, a tiny toy car, and a fortune cookie. Hide the items in the bean bowl. Have a blindfolded friend reach into the bowl and guess what they are.

make music

21 Make a drum. Turn a pail upside down. Turn a pot upside down. Turn anything upside down, and tap out rhythms using chopsticks.

22 Clap to the rhythm by slapping two disposable plastic picnic plates back to back.

23 Make a tube kazoo. Place a square piece of waxed paper over the end of a toilet-paper or paper-towel tube, and secure it in place with a rubber band. Hum and toot your favorite tunes into the tube.

24 Make a comb kazoo. Wrap a piece of waxed paper around a plastic comb. Hold the covered comb spine to your lips and hum a tune.

25 Make a jingle-bell bracelet. String 4 or 5 jingle bells onto 1 or 2 pipe cleaners and twist the ends together. Wear the bracelet on your wrist, hold and shake it like a tambourine, or tie it around an ankle to make dancing music.

26 Add a musical message to the telephone answering machine.

27 Make a shoe-box guitar. Stretch 4 or 5 large rubber bands lengthwise around an open shoe box. What happens when you vary the widths of the rubber bands? If you use shorter bands, what happens to the sound?

28 Make a maraca and shake out a beat! Put a few tablespoons of dried beans into an empty oatmeal carton and tape it shut. Or fill a plastic box with paper clips.

29 Make two maracas or shakers, using 2 small jars filled with a few tablespoons of dry beans or rice. (Don't forget to tighten the lids.)

30 Have a family karaoke night, and sing along with your favorite CDs.

31 Play a repeat-the-beat game. As one person taps, shakes, or toots out a simple rhythm, the rest of the players try to repeat the rhythm. Make each new rhythm a little longer.

32 Record family jam sessions, and sing along on a tape recorder.

in the garden

33 Fill a bucket with ice cubes, and water the sturdy plants slowly.

34 Fill a bucket with ice cubes, hide them around the yard, then play ice-cube hunt with a friend.

35 Play with a portable sandbox made from a wheelbarrow filled with sandbox sand. (You stand beside it and don't get sandy.)

36 Garden alongside the grown-ups with a bucket of kid-sized garden tools.

37 Look for volunteer seedlings in the garden or on the lawn before it's mowed. Transplant to a safe place and watch them grow.

38 Lie on the lawn and see how many letters of the alphabet you and your friends can imitate. One person can outstretch her hands to form a "T" or curl into a "C." Two can make an "X." What can three kids do? (Answer: capital "F," "H," "I," "K," "N," "Y," and "Z.")

"What can I do now?"

39 Have a scavenger hunt. You might include on your list a curly twig, a rock with holes, 4 different leaves, an ant, a worm, and a feather.

outdoors

40 Paint the sidewalk with a bucket of water and a wide brush.

41 Dip your feet in water, and leave footprints on the pavement.

42 Jump rope.

43 Blow giant bubbles using a bent wire coat hanger and an upside-down trash can lid.

44 Blow little bubbles using an open paper clip as a wand.

45 Fill a clean, empty squirt bottle, and practice your sharpshooting.

(To make a bubble solution, combine 3 cups water, 1 cup dishwashing liquid, and 6 tablespoons light corn syrup.)

on a walk

46 Use sidewalk chalk to (a) make a racetrack for toy cars; (b) play hopscotch; (c) draw animals and ABCs; and (d) write a "Welcome" message in front of your house.

47 Plant an egg-carton garden. Add potting soil and plant with parsley, chive, or nasturtium seeds. Water, and put the garden on your kitchen window sill. Keep the soil moist over the next few weeks, and see your tiny garden start to grow.

48 Watch the sunset.

49 Take an empty egg carton along and fill it with pebbles, pretty leaves, and tiny flowers to make a nature treasure chest. Or, make your walk a scavenger hunt.

50 Count the clouds, and search for interesting shapes, animals, and faces. Make up a story about them.

51 Blow off the seeds from a dandelion puff, and make a wish.

52 Whistle with a blade of grass stretched between your fingers.

53 Play "loves me, loves me not" with a petaled flower.

54 Take a Hansel and Gretel walk. On a walk with a grown-up, tie bits of string to branches along the way. Then, follow the trail home, untying the strings as you go.

help around the house

55 Find out if you can make your bed faster (and neater) than your mom can make hers.

56 Be a Super-Duper Stuff Finder. Carry a bucket around the house to see how many things you can find that belong in your room.

57 Make your own to-do list.

58 Wind up a musical toy, and see how many T-shirts you can fold or magazines you can tidy before it completely unwinds.

"what can I do now?"

59 Learn the Magic Minute. Have someone tell you when a minute begins and when it ends. Then pick a chore, such as matching clean socks. See if you can guess ahead of time how many socks you can match in a minute, then set a timer and go! (Other chores might include setting the table or stacking a week's worth of newspapers.)

60 Make a dust puppet from an old sock, and dust your room.

61 Be the Sweet Dream Elf, and put a little note, a tiny prize, or a night-night nibble on everyone's pillow.

in the car

62 Buckle your seat belt, with or without a grown-up's help.

63 Count the stop signs from here to there.

64 Count the red cars from there to here.

65 Make up some riddles and rhymes.

66 Make up new words to your favorite song.

67 Play "I Spy," and let others in the car try to guess by asking "yes" or "no" questions.

68 Play 20 Questions, and let others in the car try to guess by asking "yes" or "no" questions.

at the grocery store

69 Help put the groceries in the cart, counting them as you go.

70 Name or spell fruits and vegetables.

71 Help pick out the ingredients for trail mix from the bulk bins.

72 Play ABC Bingo. Check labels and signs to find the letters from A to Z.

73 Visit the lobster tank.

74 Count backwards from 100.

in bed with the lights out

75 Play flashlight games in the dark (see page 90).

76 Listen to music or a story on tape.

77 Tell your favorite teddy bear a bedtime story.

78 Sing your toys a good-night song.

79 Build an in-the-bed pillow fort, and cuddle up.

"What can I eat?"

1 Cut a banana in half lengthwise, and spread with peanut butter. Dot with raisins or chocolate chips.

2 Do the same thing with a whole stalk of celery.

3 Make a fast pizza by spreading an English muffin with tomato paste and grated cheese. Broil in the toaster oven until bubbly.

4 Wrap a pre-cut slice of cheese around an apple chunk. Try this with other fruit.

5 Wrap a pre-cut slice of meat around an apple chunk. Try this with other fruit.

6 Cover your fingertips with pitted olives, and eat them one by one.

7 Cover half a toasted bagel with cream cheese or peanut butter. Make a face, using blueberries for eyes, chopped nuts for freckles, shredded unpeeled red apple for hair, and a red grape for the mouth. Decorate some more with squeezable cheese, ketchup, or mustard.

8 Make a favorite smoothie recipe (see page 36) and pour the mixture into small paper cups. Cover with aluminum foil, insert a craft stick into the cup through the foil, and freeze for several hours.

9 Eat foods that begin with the letter "B."

10 Eat foods that spell your name. (For lunch I ate a Sandwich, Apple, Raspberry, and Apricot.)

11 Dunk fresh strawberries in melted chocolate chips. (Microwave ½ cup chocolate chips in a glass bowl for about 1 minute. Stir until smooth.)

12 Dip pretzel rods into melted chocolate chips, then roll in a rimmed plate of candy sprinkles.

13 Dunk fresh strawberries in light sour cream or plain yogurt, then dip in a container of brown sugar.

14 Put a scoop of frozen yogurt or ice cream between 2 graham crackers or 2 flat, round cookies.

15 Make a fruit kabob using bamboo skewers and canned pineapple chunks, cantaloupe balls, and sliced bananas. Think of other fruits you can use.

16 Top a toaster waffle with yogurt and granola, or sliced fruit and honey, or applesauce and cinnamon sugar, or even peanut butter and jelly.

17 Dip apple wedges, pear slices, celery sticks, and crackers into peanut butter thinned with honey.

18 Use cookie-cutters to cut cheese slices into fun shapes. Place them on crackers, and eat.

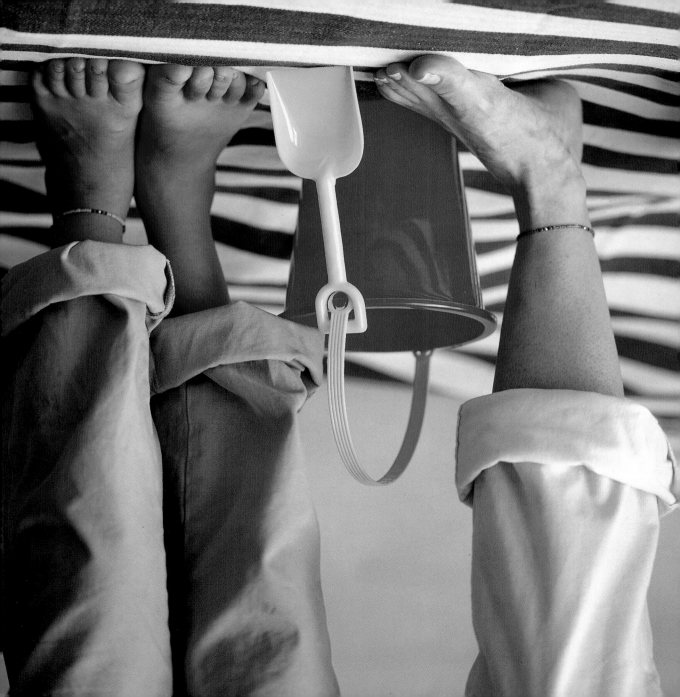

supplies

Before the weekend, take some time to check your supplies of food and crafts. You don't want to find yourself missing a crucial item halfway through a project or recipe. Here are some handy basic lists, with tasty and fun extras, to help you get organized and keep your cupboards filled and ready for just about anything.

basics:

baking supplies

baking powder and soda

butter, margarine, and vegetable shortening

chocolate: chips, unsweetened chocolate, and cocoa

dried herbs and spices

flour and Bisquick

food coloring

oil: olive, vegetable, and nonstick spray

salt and pepper

sugar: brown and white

vanilla extract

vinegar

beverages/mixes

everyone's favorites: carbonated drinks and fruit juices

adult classics: coffee, tea, wine, and beer

boxed/canned/jarred/ and wrapped goods

cereals and oatmeal

bread: sandwich

broths and soups

canned fruits and vegetables

canned tomatoes: whole, crushed, sauce, and paste

jam, jellies, and honey

mayonnaise or sandwich spread

pasta and rice

peanut butter

condiments

ketchup

mustard: Dijon and yellow (red and purple!)

olives, pickles, and pickle relish

dairy products

cheese

eggs

ice cream and frozen yogurt

milk

yogurt

fresh goods

fruits, vegetables, and salad greens

meat, poultry, and fish

tasty extras:

bagel, English muffin, pita, crackers, and croutons

candy, cookies, cakes, and marshmallows

half-and-half, sour cream, and whipping cream

decorative frostings, gels, sugars, and sprinkles

deli meats, dips, dressings, and salsas

dessert sauces and syrups: fudge, caramel, and maple

popcorn, pretzels, chips, and nuts

sauces: marinara, pizza, and spaghetti

the artbox

basics:

- adhesive tapes: clear and masking
- cookie-cutters
- cotton balls and swabs
- crayons
- felt-tipped pens and markers
- gesso
- glues: craft, white, and stick
- hot glue gun and sticks
- paintbrushes
- paints: acrylic, tempera, and water
- paper clips
- paper lunch sacks
- paper plates
- paper punch
- paper: card stock, construction, and tissue
- pencils
- plastic storage bags
- rubber bands
- ruler
- scissors
- spring-style clothespins
- wooden skewers, toothpicks, and Popsicle sticks

fun stuff:

- beads, buttons, and sequins; assorted
- corks
- decorative stickers, variety of sizes and themes
- drinking straws
- fabric paints with applicator tips
- felt squares
- glitter glues
- glitter spray
- glitters
- ribbons: curling, satin, and grosgrain
- wiggle eyes
- rubber stamps
- pipe cleaners

index